Travellers' German

David Ellis is Director of the Somerset Language Centre
and co-author of a number of language books

Annette Cheyne was born near Düsseldorf and now lives in London
and teaches German to businessmen

Dr John Baldwin is a Lecturer in Phonetics at
University College, London

Other titles in the series

Travellers' German

D. L. Ellis, A. Cheyne

Pronunciation Dr J. Baldwin

Pan Books London and Sydney

The publishers would like to thank the
Austrian, German and Swiss National Tourist Offices for their help
during the preparation of this book

First published 1981 by Pan Books Ltd,
Cavaye Place, London SW10 9PG
© D. L. Ellis and A. Cheyne 1981
ISBN 0 330 26293 9
Printed and bound in Great Britain by
Hunt Barnard Printing Ltd., Aylesbury, Bucks.

Contents

6/Contents

Using the phrase book

- Though primarily designed to help you get by in Germany, to get what you want or need, this phrase book would also be of use to travellers to Austria and Switzerland. It concentrates on the simplest but most effective way you can express these needs in an unfamiliar language.
- The CONTENTS on p. 5 give you a good idea of which section to consult for the phrase you need.
- The INDEX on p. 155 gives more detailed information about where to look for your phrase.
- When you have found the right page you will be given:
  - either – the exact phrase
  - or – help in making up a suitable sentence
  - and – help in getting the pronunciation right
- The English sentences in **bold type** will be useful for you in a variety of different situations, so they are worth learning by heart. (See also DO IT YOURSELF, p. 145.)
- Wherever possible you will find help in understanding what German people say to *you*, in reply to your questions.
- If you want to practise the basic nuts and bolts of the language further, look at the DO IT YOURSELF section starting on p. 145.
- Note especially these three sections:
  - Everyday expressions p. 11
  - Shop talk p. 57
  - Public notices p. 123
  - You are sure to want to refer to them most frequently.
- Once abroad, remember to make good use of the local tourist offices (see p. 24).

UK addresses:

Austrian National Tourist Office
30 St George Street, London W1

German National Tourist Office
61 Conduit Street, London W1

Swiss National Tourist Office
The Swiss Centre,
1 New Coventry Street, London W1

A note on the pronunciation system

It is usual in phrase books for there to be a pronunciation section, which tries to teach English-speaking tourists how to pronounce correctly the language of the country they are visiting. Such attempts are based on the argument that correct pronunciation is essential for comprehension. The system in this book, however, is founded on three quite different assumptions: firstly, that it is not possible to describe in print the sounds of a foreign language in such a way that the English speaker with no phonetic training will produce them accurately, or even intelligibly; secondly, that perfect pronunciation is not essential for communication, and lastly that the average visitor abroad is more interested in achieving successful communication than in learning how to pronounce new speech sounds. Observation and experience have shown these assumptions to be justified. The most important characteristic of the present system, therefore, is that it makes no attempt whatsoever to teach the sounds of the other language, but uses instead the nearest English sounds to them. The sentences transcribed for pronunciation are designed to be read as naturally as possible, as if they were ordinary English (of a generally south-eastern English variety), and with no attempt to make the words sound 'foreign'. In this way you will still sound quite English, but you will at the same time be understood. Practice always helps performance, and it is a good idea to rehearse aloud any of the sentences you know you are going to need. When you do come to the point of using them, say them with conviction.

In German it is important to stress or emphasize the syllables in italics, just as you would if we were to take as an English example: *li*ttle Jack *Hor*ner *sa*t in the *cor*ner. Here we have ten syllables, but only four stresses.

Of course you may enjoy trying to pronounce a foreign language as well as possible and the present system is a good way to start. However, since it uses only the sounds of English, you will very soon need to depart from it as you imitate the sounds you hear the native speaker produce and begin to relate them to the spelling of the other language. German will pose no problems as there is an obvious and consistent relationship between pronunciation and spelling.

Viel Spass!

John Baldwin, 1980

1 SCHLESWIG – HOLSTEIN
2 HAMBURG
3 LOWER SAXONY
4 BREMEN
5 NORTH RHINE – WESTPHALIA
6 HESSE
7 RHINELAND – PALATINATE
8 SAARLAND
9 BADEN – WÜR HEMBURG
10 BAVARIA
11 BERLIN (WEST)

Everyday expressions

[See also 'Shop talk', p. 57]

Hello	**Guten Tag** goo-ten tahk
Hello (Austria)	**Grüss Gott** grooss got
Good morning	**Guten Morgen** goo-ten morgen
Good day Good afternoon]	**Guten Tag** goo-ten tahk
Good evening	**Guten Abend** goo-ten ah-bent
Good night	**Gute Nacht** goo-teh nakt
Good-bye	⎡**Auf Wiedersehn** owf veeder-zain **Tschüss** (friends only) ⎣choos
See you later	**Bis später** bis shpater
Yes	**Ja** yah
Please	**Bitte** bitteh
Yes, please	**Ja, bitte** yah bitteh
Great!	**Prima!** pree-mah
Thank you	**Danke** dankeh
Thank you very much	**Vielen Dank** feelen dank
That's right	**Das stimmt** das shtimmt
No	**Nein** nine
No, thank you	**Nein, danke** nine dankeh
I disagree	**Das stimmt nicht** das shtimmt nisht

Excuse me Sorry	**Entschuldigen Sie** ent-sh*oo*l-dig-en zee
Don't mention it That's OK	**Bitte sehr** b*i*tteh zair
That's good I like it	**Das gefällt mir** das ga-f*e*llt meer
That's no good I don't like it	**Das gefällt mir nicht** das ga-f*e*llt meer n*i*sht
I know	**Ich weiss** ish v*i*ce
I don't know	**Ich weiss nicht** ish v*i*ce nisht
It doesn't matter	**Es macht nichts** es m*a*kt n*i*shts
Where's the toilet, please?	**Wo sind die Toiletten?** v*o* zint dee twa-l*e*tten
How much is that? [*point*]	**Wieviel kostet das?** vee-feel k*o*stet das
Is the service included?	**Ist die Bedienung inbegriffen?** ist dee bed*ee*-noong *i*n-beg-riffen
Do you speak English?	**Sprechen Sie Englisch?** shpr*e*shen zee *e*ng-lish
I'm sorry . . .	**Es tut mir leid . . .** es t*oo*t meer l*i*te . . .
I don't speak German	**ich spreche nicht Deutsch** ish shpr*e*sheh nisht d*o*ytsh
I only speak a little German	**ich spreche nur ein wenig Deutsch** ish shpr*e*sheh noor ine v*ay*-nik d*o*ytsh
I don't understand	**ich verstehe nicht** ish fer-sht*ay*-heh nisht
Please can you . . .	**Bitte können Sie . . .** b*i*tteh k*e*rnnen zee . . .
repeat that?	**das wiederholen?** das v*ee*der-holen
speak more slowly?	**langsamer sprechen?** l*a*ng-zahmer shpr*e*shen
write it down?	**das aufschreiben?** das *o*wf-shry-ben
What is this called in German? [*point*]	**Wie heisst das auf Deutsch?** vee h*y*sst das owf d*o*ytsh

Crossing the border

ESSENTIAL INFORMATION

- Don't waste time just before you leave rehearsing what you're going to say to the border officials – the chances are that you won't have to say anything at all, especially if you travel by air.
- It's more useful to check that you have your documents handy for the journey: passport, tickets, money, travellers' cheques, insurance documents, driving licence and car registration documents.
- Look out for these signs:
  ZOLL   (customs)
  GRENZE   (border)
  GRENZPOLIZEI (frontier police)
  [*For further signs and notices, see p. 123*]
- You may be asked routine questions by the customs officials [*see below*]. If you have to give personal details see 'Meeting people', p. 15. The other most important answer to know is 'Nothing': **Nichts** (nishts).

ROUTINE QUESTIONS

Passport?	**Pass?**
	pass
Insurance?	**Versicherungskarte?**
	fer-zisher-oongs-karteh
Registration document? (logbook)	**Kraftfahrzeugschein?**
	kraft-far-tsoyk-shine
Ticket, please	**Fahrkarte, bitte**
	far-karteh bitteh
Have you anything to declare?	**Haben Sie etwas zu verzollen?**
	hahben zee etvas tsoo fer-tsollen
Where are you going?	**Wohin fahren Sie?**
	vo-hin far-en zee
How long are you staying?	**Wie lange bleiben Sie?**
	vee lang-eh bly-ben zee
Where have you come from?	**Woher kommen Sie?**
	vo-hair kommen zee

You may also have to fill in forms which ask for:

surname	(Familien–) Name
first name	Vorname
maiden name	Mädchenname
place of birth	Geburtsort
date of birth	Geburtsdatum
address	Adresse/Anschrift
nationality	Staatsangehörigkeit
profession	Beruf
passport number	Passnummer
issued at	ausgestellt in
signature	Unterschrift

Meeting people

[*See also 'Everyday expressions', p. 11*]

Breaking the ice

Hello	**Guten Tag (Hallo)**
	g*oo*-ten tahk (hullo)
Hello (Austria)	**Grüss Gott**
	grooss got
Good morning	**Guten Morgen**
	g*oo*-ten morgen
How are you?	**Wie geht es Ihnen? (Wie geht's?)**
	vee g*ai*t es *ee*n*è*n (vee g*ai*ts)

[*Expressions above in brackets should only be used with people you know well.*]

Pleased to meet you	**Angenehm**
	*u*n-ga-name
I am here ...	**Ich bin hier ...**
	ish bin here ...
on holiday	**auf Urlaub**
	owf *oo*r-lowp
on business	**auf Geschäftsreise**
	owf gash*e*fts-ryzeh
Can I offer you ...	**Kann ich Ihnen ... anbieten?**
	kan ish *ee*nen ... *a*n-beeten
a drink?	**etwas zu trinken**
	*e*tvas tsoo tr*i*nken
a cigarette?	**eine Zigarette**
	*i*neh tsee-gar*e*tteh
a cigar?	**eine Zigarre**
	*i*neh tsee-g*a*rreh
Are you staying long?	**Bleiben Sie hier lang?**
	bly-ben zee here l*a*ng-eh

Name

What's your name?	**Wie ist Ihr Name?**
	vee ist eer n*a*hmeh
My name is ...	**Mein Name ist ...**
	mine n*a*hmeh ist ...

Family

Are you married?	**Sind Sie verheiratet?**
	zint zee fer-hy-rah-tet
I am ...	**Ich bin ...**
	ish bin ...
married	**verheiratet**
	fer-hy-rah-tet
single	**ledig**
	laid-ik
This is ...	**Dies ist ...**
	dees ist ...
my wife	**meine Frau**
	mineh frow
my husband	**mein Mann**
	mine munn
my son	**mein Sohn**
	mine zone
my daughter	**meine Tochter**
	mineh tokter
my (boy) friend	**mein Freund**
	mine froynt
my (girl) friend	**meine Freundin**
	mineh froyndin
my (male) colleague	**mein Kollege**
	mine col-laig-eh
my (female) colleague	**meine Kollegin**
	mineh col-laig-in
Do you have any children?	**Haben Sie Kinder?**
	hahben zee kin-der
I have ...	**Ich habe ...**
	ish hahbeh ...
one daughter	**eine Tochter**
	ineh toshter
one son	**einen Sohn**
	inen zone
two daughters	**zwei Töchter**
	tsvy tershter
three sons	**drei Söhne**
	dry zerneh
No, I haven't any children	**Nein, ich habe keine Kinder**
	nine ish hahbeh kineh kin-der

Where you live

Are you ...	**Sind Sie ...**
	zint zee ...
German?	**Deutscher/Deutsche?***
	doyt-sher/doyt-sheh
Austrian?	**Österreicher/Österreicherin?***
	erster-ryker/erster-ryker-in
Swiss?	**Schweizer/Schweizerin?***
	shvytser/shvytser-in
I am ...	**Ich bin ...**
	ish bin ...
American	**Amerikaner/Amerikanerin***
	ameri-kah-ner/ameri-kah-ner-in
English	**Engländer/Engländerin***
	eng-lender/eng-lender-in

[*For other nationalities, see p. 138*]

* For men use the first word, for women the second.

Where are you from?

I'm ...	**Ich bin ...**
	ish bin ...
from London	**aus London**
	ows london
from England	**aus England**
	ows eng-lant
from the north	**aus dem Norden**
	ows dem norden
from the south	**aus dem Süden**
	ows dem zooden
from the east	**aus dem Osten**
	ows dem osten
from the west	**aus dem Westen**
	ows dem vesten
from the centre	**aus dem Zentrum (des Landes)**
	ows dem tsent-room (des land-es)

[*For other countries, see p. 137*]

For the businessman and woman

I'm from ... (firm's name)
Ich bin von ...
ish bin fon ...

I have an appointment with ...
Ich habe eine Verabredung mit ...
ish hahbeh ineh fer-up-ray-doong mit ...

May I speak to ...?
Kann ich ... sprechen?
kan ish ... shpreshen

This is my card
Hier ist meine Karte
here ist mineh karteh

I'm sorry, I'm late
Es tut mir leid, ich habe mich verspätet
es toot meer lite ish hahbeh mish fer-shpay-tet

Can I fix another appointment?
Kann ich eine neue Verabredung treffen?
kan ish ineh noy-eh fer-up-ray-doong treffen

I'm staying at the (Crown) hotel
Ich wohne im Hotel (Krone)
ish vone-eh im hotel (krone-eh)

I'm staying in (Park) Road
Ich wohne in der (Park) strasse
ish vone-eh in der (park) shtrahsseh

Asking the way

ESSENTIAL INFORMATION

- Keep a look out for all these place names as you will find them on shops, maps and notices.

WHAT TO SAY

Excuse me, please	**Entschuldigen Sie, bitte** ent-shool-dig-en zee bitteh
How do I get ...	**Wie komme ich ...** vee kommeh ish ...
to Hamburg?	**nach Hamburg?** nahk hum-boork
to (Station) Road?	**zur (Bahnhof)strasse?** tsoor (bahn-hof-)shtrahsseh
to the hotel (Krone)?	**zum Hotel (Krone)?** tsoom hotel (krone-eh)
to the airport?	**zum Flughafen?** tsoom flook-hahfen
to the beach?	**zum Strand?** tsoom shtrant
to the bus station?	**zum Busbahnhof?** tsoom boos-bahn-hof
to the historic site?	**zur historischen Stätte?** tsoor histo-rish-en shtetteh
to the market?	**zum Markt?** tsoom markt
to the police station?	**zur Polizeiwache** tsoor poli-tsy-vakkeh
to the port?	**zum Hafen?** tsoom hahfen
to the post office?	**zum Postamt?** tsoom post-amt
to the railway station?	**zum Bahnhof?** tsoom bahn-hof
to the sports stadium?	**zum Stadion?** tsoom shtah-dee-on

How do I get ...	**Wie komme ich ...**
	vee *k*omme*h* ish ...
to the tourist information office?	**zum Fremdenverkehrsbüro?**
	tsoom fremden-ferkairs-bur*o*
to the town centre?	**zum Stadtzentrum?**
	tsoom sht*a*tt-tsent-room
to the town hall?	**zum Rathaus?**
	tsoom r*a*ht-house
Excuse me, please	**Entschuldigen Sie, bitte**
	ent-sh*oo*l-dig-en zee b*i*tteh
Is there ... near by?	**Gibt es ... in der Nähe?**
	geept es ... in der n*a*y-eh
an art gallery	**eine Kunstgalerie**
	*i*neh k*oo*nst-galer*ee*
a baker's	**eine Bäckerei**
	*i*neh becker-*ry*
a bank	**eine Bank**
	*i*neh b*a*nk
a bar	**eine Bar**
	*i*neh b*a*r
a botanical garden	**einen botanischen Garten**
	*i*nen bot*a*h-nishen g*a*rten
a bus stop	**eine Bushaltestelle**
	*i*neh b*oo*s-halteh-shtelleh
a butcher's	**eine Metzgerei**
	*i*neh mets-ga-r*y*
a café	**ein Café**
	ine caff*ay*
a cake shop	**eine Konditorei**
	*i*neh con-dee-to-r*y*
a campsite	**einen Campingplatz**
	*i*nen c*a*mping-plats
a car park	**einen Parkplatz**
	*i*nen p*a*rk-plats
a change bureau	**eine Wechselstube**
	*i*neh v*e*ksel-shtoobeh
a chemist's	**eine Apotheke**
	*i*neh ah-pot*a*ke-eh
a church	**eine Kirche**
	*i*neh k*eer*-sheh
a cinema	**ein Kino**
	ine k*ee*-no

a delicatessen	**ein Feinkostgeschäft** *i*ne f*i*ne-kost-gash*e*ft
a dentist's	**einen Zahnarzt** *i*nen ts*a*hn-artst
a department store	**ein Kaufhaus** ine k*o*wf-house
a disco	**eine Diskothek** *i*neh disco-t*a*ke
a doctor's surgery	**eine Arztpraxis** *i*neh *a*rtst-prak-sis
a dry cleaner's	**eine Reinigung** *i*neh r*y*-nee-goong
a fishmonger's	**ein Fischgeschäft** ine f*i*sh-gash*e*ft
a garage (for repairs)	**eine Autowerkstatt** *i*neh *o*wto-vairk-shtatt
a hairdresser's	**einen Frisör** *i*nen free-z*e*r
a greengrocer's	**eine Gemüsehandlung** *i*neh ga-m*oo*zeh-hant-loong
a grocer's	**ein Lebensmittelgeschäft** ine l*a*bens-mittel-gash*e*ft
a hardware shop	**eine Eisenwarenhandlung** *i*neh *i*zen-vahren-handloong
a hospital	**ein Krankenhaus** ine kr*a*nken-house
a hotel	**ein Hotel** ine hotel
an ice-cream parlour	**eine Eisdiele** *i*neh *i*ce-deeleh
a local sickness insurance office	**eine Krankenkasse** *i*neh kr*a*nken-kasseh
a laundry	**eine Wäscherei** *i*neh vesheh-r*y*
a museum	**ein Museum** ine moo-z*a*y-oom
a newsagent's	**einen Zeitungshändler** *i*nen ts*y*-toongs-hentler
a night club	**einen Nachtklub** *i*nen n*a*kt-kloop
a park	**einen Park** *i*nen p*a*rk

Is there . . . near by?　　　**Gibt es . . . in der Nähe?**
　　　　　　　　　　　　　　　geept es . . . in der n*ay*-eh

a petrol station	**eine Tankstelle**
	*i*neh t*a*nk-shtelleh
a post box	**einen Briefkasten**
	*i*nen br*ee*f-kasten
a public toilet	**öffentliche Toiletten**
	erffent-lish-eh twa-letten
a restaurant	**ein Restaurant**
	ine rest-o-r*u*ng
a snack bar	**einen Schnellimbiss**
	*i*nen shn*e*ll-im-bis
a sports ground	**einen Sportplatz**
	*i*nen shport-plats
a supermarket	**einen Supermarkt**
	*i*nen z*oo*per-markt
a sweet shop	**einen Süsswarenladen**
	*i*nen z*oo*ss-vahren-lahden
a swimming pool	**ein Schwimmbad**
	ine shv*i*mm-baht
a taxi stand	**einen Taxistand**
	*i*nen t*a*xi-shtant
a telephone	**eine Telefonzelle**
	*i*neh telef*o*ne-tselleh
a theatre	**ein Theater**
	ine tay-*a*hter
a tobacconist's	**einen Zigarettenladen**
	*i*nen tsee-gar*e*tten-lahden
a travel agent's	**ein Reisebüro**
	ine r*y*zeh-buro
a youth hostel	**eine Jugendherberge**
	*i*neh y*oo*gent-hair-bairgeh
a zoo	**einen Zoo**
	*i*nen ts*o*

DIRECTIONS

- Asking where a place is, or if a place is near by, is one thing; making sense of the answer is another.
- Here are some of the most important key directions and replies.

Left	**Links**
	links
Right	**Rechts**
	reshts
Straight on	**Geradeaus**
	grahdeh-*ows*
There	**Dort**
	dort
First left/right	**Erste Strasse links/rechts**
	*air*steh sht*r*ahsseh *l*inks/*r*eshts
Second left/right	**Zweite Strasse links/ rechts**
	tsv*y*-teh sht*r*ahsseh *l*inks/*r*eshts
At the crossroads	**Bei der Kreuzung**
	by der kr*oy*-tsoong
At the traffic lights	**Bei der Ampel**
	by der *u*mpel
At the roundabout	**Beim Kreisverkehr**
	bime kr*i*ce-fer-kair
At the level-crossing	**Beim Bahnübergang**
	bime b*a*hn-oober-gang
It's near/far	**Es ist nah/weit**
	es ist n*a*h/v*i*te
One kilometre	**Ein Kilometer**
	ine kilo-m*a*ter
Two kilometres	**Zwei Kilometer**
	tsvy kilo-m*a*ter
Five minutes ...	**Fünf Minuten ...**
	foonf min*oo*ten ...
on foot	**zu Fuss**
	tsoo f*oo*ss
by car	**mit dem Auto**
	mit dem *o*wto
Take ...	**Nehmen Sie ...**
	n*ay*-men zee ...
the bus	**den Bus**
	den b*oo*ss
the train	**den Zug**
	den ts*oo*k
the tram	**die Strassenbahn**
	dee sht*r*ahssen-bahn
the underground	**die U–Bahn**
[For public transport, see	dee *oo*-bahn
p. 114]	

The tourist information office

ESSENTIAL INFORMATION

- Most towns and holiday resorts in Germany, Switzerland and Austria have a tourist information office; in smaller towns the local travel agent (**REISEBÜRO**) provides the same information and services.
- Look for these words:
  FREMDENVERKEHRSBÜRO
  VERKEHRSAMT
  INFORMATIONSBÜRO
- If your main concern is to find and book accommodation, a **ZIMMERNACHWEIS** (room-booking office) is the best place to go to.
- Tourist offices offer you free information in the form of printed leaflets, fold-outs, brochures, lists and plans.
- You may have to pay for some types of documents but this is not usual.
- For finding a tourist office, see p. 19.

WHAT TO SAY

Please, have you got . . .	**Bitte, haben Sie . . .** b*i*tteh h*a*hben zee . . .
a plan of the town?	**einen Stadtplan?** *i*nen sht*a*tt-plahn
a list of events?	**einen Veranstaltungskalender** *i*nen fer-*u*n-shtaltoongs-kal*e*nder
a list of hotels?	**ein Hotelverzeichnis?** ine hot*e*l-fer-tsysh-nis
a list of campsites?	**ein Campingplatzverzeichnis?** ine camping-plats-fer-tsysh-nis
a list of restaurants?	**ein Restaurantverzeichnis?** ine resto-r*u*ng-fer-tsysh-nis
a list of coach excursions?	**eine Liste mit Ausflugsfahrten?** *i*neh l*i*steh mit *o*ws-flooks-farten
a leaflet on the town?	**einen Prospekt von dieser Stadt?** *i*nen pro-sp*e*kt fon d*ee*zer sht*a*tt

a leaflet on the region?	**einen Prospekt von dieser Gegend?**
	inen pro-spekt fon deezer gay-ghent
a railway timetable?	**einen Zugfahrplan?**
	inen tsook-far-plahn
a bus timetable?	**einen Busfahrplan?**
	inen booss-far-plahn
In English, please	**Auf Englisch, bitte**
	owf eng-lish bitteh
How much do I owe you?	**Wieviel schulde ich Ihnen?**
	vee-feel shooldeh ish eenen
Can you recommend . . .	**Können Sie . . . empfehlen?**
	kernnen zee . . . em-pfailen
a cheap hotel?	**ein billiges Hotel**
	ine billig-es hotel
a cheap restaurant?	**ein billiges Restaurant**
	ine billig-es resto-rung
Can you make a booking for me?	**Können Sie eine Reservierung für mich machen?**
	kernnen zee ineh reser-vee-roong foor mish makhen

LIKELY ANSWERS

You need to understand when the answer is 'No'. You should be able to tell by the assistant's facial expression, tone of voice and gesture, but there are some language clues, such as:

No	**Nein**
	nine
I'm sorry	**(Es) tut mir leid**
	(es) toot meer lite
I don't have a list of campsites	**Ich habe kein Campingplatzverzeichnis**
	ish hahbeh kine camping-plats-fer-tsysh-nis
I haven't got any left	**Ich habe keine mehr**
	ish hahbeh kineh mair
It's free	**Es ist umsonst**
	es ist oom-zonst

Accommodation

Hotel

ESSENTIAL INFORMATION

- If you want hotel-type accommodation, all the following words in capital letters are worth looking for on name boards:
  HOTEL
  HOTEL GARNI (room and breakfast, no other meals provided)
  MOTEL
  PENSION (boarding house)
  GASTHOF (inexpensive type of inn with a limited number of rooms)
  ZIMMER FREI (rooms to let in private houses, bed and breakfast)
- A list of hotels in the town or district can usually be obtained at the local tourist information office [see p. 24].
- Unlisted hotels are usually slightly cheaper and probably almost as good as listed hotels.
- Not all hotels and boarding-houses provide meals apart from breakfast; inquire about this, on arrival, at the reception.
- The cost is displayed in the room itself, so you can check it when having a look round before agreeing to stay.
- The displayed cost is for the room itself, per night and not per person. It usually includes service charges and taxes, but quite often does not include breakfast.
- Breakfast is continental style, with rolls, butter and jam; boiled eggs, cheese and cold meats are usually available on request. Some larger hotels also offer a FRÜHSTÜCKS-BUFFET where you can help yourself to cereals, yoghurt, fresh fruit etc.
- Upon arrival you will have to fill in the official registration form which bears an English translation. The receptionist will also want to see your passport.
- It is customary to tip the porter and leave a tip for the chambermaid in the hotel room.
- Finding a hotel, see p. 19.

WHAT TO SAY

I have a booking	**Ich habe reserviert**
	ish h*a*hbeh reserv*ee*rt
Have you any vacancies, please?	**Haben Sie noch Zimmer frei?**
	h*a*hben zee nok ts*i*mmer fry
Can I book a room?	**Kann ich ein Zimmer reservieren lassen?**
	kan ish ine ts*i*mmer reser-v*ee*ren l*a*ssen
It's for ...	**Es ist für ...**
	es ist foor ...
one person	**eine Person**
	*i*neh per-z*o*ne
two people	**zwei Personen**
[*For numbers, see p. 129*]	tsvy per-z*o*nen
It's for ...	**Es ist für ...**
	es ist foor ...
one night	**eine Nacht**
	*i*neh n*a*kt
two nights	**zwei Nächte**
	tsvy n*e*sh-teh
one week	**eine Woche**
	*i*neh v*o*k-eh
two weeks	**zwei Wochen**
	tsvy v*o*kken
I would like ...	**Ich möchte ...**
	ish m*e*rshteh ...
a room	**ein Zimmer**
	ine ts*i*mmer
two rooms	**zwei Zimmer**
	tsvy ts*i*mmer
a room with a single bed	**ein Einzelzimmer**
	ine *i*ne-tsel-tsimmer
a room with two single beds	**ein Zweibettzimmer**
	ine tsv*y*-bett-tsimmer
a room with a double bed	**ein Doppelzimmer**
	ine doppel-tsimmer
I would like a room ...	**Ich möchte ein Zimmer ...**
	ish m*e*rshteh ine ts*i*mmer ...
with a toilet	**mit Toilette**
	mit twa- letteh

I would like a room ...	**Ich möchte ein Zimmer ...**
	ish mershteh ine tsimmer ...
with a bathroom	**mit Bad**
	mit baht
with a shower	**mit Dusche**
	mit doo-sheh
with a cot	**mit einem Kinderbett**
	mit inem kin-der-bett
with a balcony	**mit Balkon**
	mit bal-kone
I would like ...	**Ich möchte ...**
	ish mershteh ...
full board	**Vollpension**
	foll-penzee-on
half board	**Halbpension**
	hal-penzee-on
bed and breakfast [see Essential information]	**Übernachtung mit Frühstück**
	oober-naktoong mit froo-shtok
Do you serve meals?	**Kann man bei Ihnen essen?**
	kan man by eenen essen
At what time is ...	**Wann gibt es ...**
	vann geept es ...
breakfast?	**Frühstück?**
	froo-shtook
lunch?	**Mittagessen?**
	mittahk-essen
dinner?	**Abendessen?**
	ahbent-essen
How much is it?	**Wieviel kostet es?**
	vee-feel kostet es
Can I look at the room?	**Kann ich mir das Zimmer ansehen?**
	kan ish meer das tsimmer un-zay-en
I'd prefer a room ...	**Ich hätte lieber ein Zimmer ...**
	ish hetteh leeber ine tsimmer ...
at the front/at the back	**nach vorn/nach hinten**
	nahk forn/nahk hin-ten
OK, I'll take it	**Gut, ich nehme es**
	goot ish nay-meh es
No thanks, I won't take it	**Nein, danke, ich nehme es nicht**
	nine dankeh ish nay-meh es nisht

The key to number (10), please
Den Schlüssel für Zimmer (Zehn), bitte
den shloossel foor tsimmer (tsain) bitteh

Please may I have ...
Kann ich bitte ... haben?
kan ish bitteh ... hahben

a coat hanger?
einen Kleiderbügel
inen klyder-boogel

a towel?
ein Handtuch
ine hant-took

a glass?
ein Glas?
ine glass

some soap?
ein Stück Seife
ine shtook zy-feh

an ashtray?
einen Aschenbecher
inen ashen-besher

another pillow?
noch ein Kopfkissen
nok ine kopf-kissen

another blanket?
noch eine Decke
nok ineh deckeh

Come in!
Herein!
her-rine

One moment, please!
Einen Moment, bitte!
inen mo-ment bitteh

Please can you ...
Bitte, können Sie ...
bitteh kernnen zee ...

do this laundry/dry cleaning?
diese Sachen waschen lassen/ reinigen lassen?
deezeh zakken vashen lassen/ ry-neeg-en lassen

call me at ... ?
mich um ... anrufen
mish oom ... un-roofen

help me with my luggage?
mir mit meinem Gepäck behilflich sein?
meer mit minem ga-peck be-hilf-lish zine

call me a taxi for ... ?
mir für ... ein Taxi bestellen?
meer foor ... ine taxi beshtellen
[*For times, see p. 131*]

The bill, please
Die Rechnung, bitte
dee resh-noong bitteh

Is service included?
Ist Bedienung inbegriffen?
ist bedee-noong in-begriffen

I think this is wrong | **Ich glaube, hier ist ein Fehler**
ish gla-oobeh here ist ine failer

May I have a receipt? | **Kann ich eine Quittung haben?**
kan ish ineh kvit-oong habben

At breakfast

Some more . . . please | **Noch etwas . . . bitte**
nok etvas . . . bitteh

  coffee | **Kaffee**
kaffeh

  tea | **Tee**
tay

  bread | **Brot**
brote

  butter | **Butter**
bootter

  jam | **Marmelade**
marmeh-lahdeh

May I have a boiled egg? | **Kann ich ein gekochtes Ei haben?**
kan ish ine gakokt-es eye habben

LIKELY REACTIONS

Have you an identity document? | **Haben Sie einen Pass oder Personalausweis?**
habben zee inen pass oder per-zonahl-ows-vice

What's your name? [see p.15] | **Wie ist Ihr Name?**
vee ist eer nahmeh

Sorry, we're full | **Es tut mir leid, wir sind ausgebucht**
es toot meer lite veer zint ows-gabookt

I haven't any rooms left | **Ich habe keine Zimmer mehr frei**
ish habbeh kineh tsimmer mair fry

Do you want to have a look? | **Wollen Sie es sich ansehen?**
vollen zee es zish un-zay-en

How many people is it for? | **Für wieviele Personen soll es sein?**
foor vee-feeleh per-zonen zoll es zine

From (7 o'clock) onwards	**Ab (sieben Uhr)** up (*zeeben oor*)
From (midday) onwards	**Ab (zwölf Uhr mittags)** up (tsverlf oor m*it*-tahks

[*For times, see p. 131*]

It's (40) marks	**Es kostet(vierzig) Mark** es k*o*stet (f*ee*r-tsik) m*ark*

[*For numbers, see p. 129*]

Camping and youth hostelling

ESSENTIAL INFORMATION

Camping

- Look for the words: **CAMPINGPLATZ ZELTPLATZ**
- Be prepared for the following charges:
  per person
  for the car (if applicable)
  for the tent or caravan plot
  for electricity
  for hot showers
- You must provide proof of identity, such as your passport.
- If you cannot find an official camping site and want to camp elsewhere, get the permission of the farmer/landowner or the local police first.
- Camping is forbidden in the lay-bys off the motorways.
- It is usually not possible to make advance reservations on camping sites. Try and secure a site in mid-afternoon if you are travelling during the high season.
- Owners of camping sites in Germany are not liable for losses. You should make your own insurance arrangements in advance.

Youth hostels

- Look for the word **JUGENDHERBERGE**.
- You must have a YHA card.
- Your YHA card must bear your photograph; you can attach it yourself, it does not require stamping.
- There is no upper age limit at German youth hostels, except in Bavaria where the age limit is twenty-seven.
- The charge for the night is the same for all ages, but some hostels are dearer than others.
- Accommodation is usually in small dormitories.
- Many German youth hostels do *not* provide a kitchen in which visitors can prepare their own meals; but usually meals at a reasonable price are provided by the house-parents.
- You may have to help with domestic chores in some hostels.
- Finding a campsite and a youth hostel, see p. 19.
- Replacing equipment, see p. 54.

WHAT TO SAY

I have a booking	**Ich habe reserviert**
	ish h*a*hbeh reserv*ee*rt
Have you any vacancies?	**Haben Sie noch etwas frei?**
	h*a*hben zee nok *e*tvas fry
It's for …	**Es ist für …**
	es ist foor
one adult/one person	**einen Erwachsenen/eine Person**
	*i*nen er-v*a*ksen-en/*i*neh per-z*o*ne
two adults/two people	**zwei Erwachsene/zwei Personen**
	tsvy er-v*a*ksen-eh/tsvy per-z*o*nen
and one child	**und ein Kind**
	oont ine kint
and two children	**und zwei Kinder**
	oont tsvy k*i*n-der
It's for …	**Es ist für …**
	es ist foor …
one night	**eine Nacht**
	*i*neh n*a*kt
two nights	**zwei Nächte**
	tsvy n*e*sh-teh

one week	**eine Woche**
	ineh vok-eh
two weeks	**zwei Wochen**
	tsvy vok-en
How much is it ...	**Wie hoch ist die Gebühr ...**
	vee hoke ist dee gaboor ...
for the tent?	**für das Zelt?**
	foor das tselt
for the caravan?	**für den Wohnwagen?**
	foor den vone-vahgen
for the car?	**für das Auto?**
	foor das owto
for the electricity?	**für Elektrizität**
	foor elektri-tsee-tate
per person?	**pro Person?**
	pro per-zone
per day/night?	**pro Tag/Nacht?**
	pro tahk/nakt
May I look round?	**Kann ich mich etwas umsehen?**
	kan ish mish etvas oom-zay-en
At what time do you lock up at night?	**Um wieviel Uhr schliessen Sie nachts ab?**
	oom vee-feel oor shleessen zee nakts up
Do you provide anything ...	**Kann man bei Ihnen etwas ... bekommen?**
	kan man by eenen etvas ... bekommen
to eat?	**zu essen**
	tsoo essen
to drink?	**zu trinken**
	tsoo trinken
Do you have ...	**Haben Sie ...**
	hahben zee ...
a bar?	**eine Bar?**
	ineh bar
hot showers?	**heisse Duschen?**
	hysseh doo-shen
a kitchen?	**eine Küche?**
	ineh koo-sheh
a launderette?	**einen Waschsalon?**
	inen vash-zalong

Do you have ...   **Haben Sie ...**
                                  h*a*hben zee ...
  a restaurant?   **ein Restaurant?**
                                  *i*ne resto-r*u*ng
  a shop?   **ein Geschäft?**
                                  *i*ne gash*e*ft
  a swimming pool?   **ein Schwimmbad?**
                                  *i*ne shv*i*mm-baht
  a snack-bar?   **eine Imbisstube?**
                                  *i*neh *i*m-bis-shtoobeh

[*For food shopping, see p. 61, and for eating and drinking out,
see p. 80*]

Where are ...   **Wo sind ...**
                                  vo zint ...
  the dustbins?   **die Abfalleimer?**
                                  dee *u*p-fall-*i*mer
  the showers?   **die Duschen?**
                                  dee d*oo*-shen
  the toilets?   **die Toiletten?**
                                  dee twa-l*e*tten
At what time must one ...   **Um wieviel Uhr muss man ...**
                                  oom v*ee*-feel oor mooss man ...
  go to bed?   **schlafen gehen?**
                                  shl*a*h-fen gain
  get up?   **aufstehen?**
                                  *o*wf-shtain
Please have you got ...   **Bitte haben Sie vielleicht ...**
                                  b*i*tteh h*a*hben zee fee-lysht ...
  a broom?   **einen Besen?**
                                  *i*nen b*a*y-zen
  a corkscrew?   **einen Korkenzieher?**
                                  *i*nen k*o*rken-tsee-er
  a drying-up cloth?   **ein Geschirrtuch?**
                                  *i*ne gash*ee*r-took
  a fork?   **eine Gabel?**
                                  *i*neh g*a*h-bel
  a fridge?   **einen Kühlschrank?**
                                  *i*nen k*oo*l-shrank

a frying pan?	**eine Bratpfanne?**
	*i*neh br*a*ht-fun-eh
an iron?	**ein Bügeleisen?**
	ine b*oo*gel-*i*zen
a knife?	**ein Messer?**
	ine m*e*sser
a plate?	**einen Teller?**
	*i*nen t*e*ller
a saucepan?	**einen Kochtopf?**
	*i*nen k*o*k-topf
a teaspoon?	**einen Teelöffel?**
	*i*nen t*a*y-lerffel
a tin opener?	**einen Dosenöffner?**
	*i*nen d*o*ze-en-erffner
any washing powder?	**Waschpulver?**
	v*a*sh-poolver
any washing-up liquid?	**ein Spülmittel?**
	ine shp*oo*l-mittel
The bill, please	**Die Rechnung, bitte**
	dee r*e*sh-noong b*i*tteh

Problems

The toilet	**Die Toilette**
	dee twa-l*e*tteh
The shower	**Die Dusche**
	dee d*oo*-sheh
The tap	**Der Wasserhahn**
	der v*a*sser-hahn
The razor point	**Die Steckdose für den Rasierapparat**
	dee sht*e*ck-doze-eh foor den raz*ee*r-app*a*raht
The light	**Das Licht**
	das l*i*sht
... is not working	**... funktioniert nicht**
	... foonk-tsee-o-n*ee*rt nisht
My camping gas has run out	**Ich habe kein Camping-Gas mehr**
	ish h*a*hbeh kine c*a*mping-gahs m*ai*r

LIKELY REACTIONS

Have you an identity document?	**Haben Sie einen Pass oder Personalausweis?** hahben zee inen pass oder per-zonahl-ows-vice
Your membership card, please	**Ihre Mitgliedskarte, bitte** eereh mit-gleets-karteh bitteh
What's your name [see p.15]	**Wie ist Ihr Name?** vee ist eer nahmeh
Sorry, we're full	**Es tut mir leid, wir sind voll besetzt** es toot meer lite veer zint foll bezetst
How many people is it for?	**Für wieviele Personen?** foor vee-feeleh per-zonen
How many nights is it for?	**Für wieviele Nächte?** foor vee-feeleh nesh-teh
It's (4) marks ...	**Es kostet (vier) Mark ...** es kostet (feer) mark ...
per day/per night	**pro Tag/pro Nacht** pro tahk/pro nakt

[For numbers, see p. 129]

Rented accommodation : problem solving

ESSENTIAL INFORMATION

- If you're looking for accommodation to rent, look out for:
  ZU VERMIETEN (to let)
  APPARTEMENTS (flats)
  FERIENWOHNUNGEN (holiday flats)
  CHALETS
- For arranging details of your let, see 'Hotel', p. 26.
- Key words you will meet if renting on the spot:
  die Kaution   deposit
  de kow-tsee-*on*
  der Schlüssel   key
  der shl*oo*ssel
- Having arranged your own accommodation and arrived with
  the key, check the obvious basics that you take for granted at
  home.
  Electricity: Voltage? Razors and small appliances brought
  from home may need adjusting. You may need an adaptor.
  Gas: Town gas or bottled gas? Butane gas must be kept in-
  doors, propane gas must be kept outdoors.
  Cooker: Don't be surprised to find:
  —the grill inside the oven, or no grill at all.
  —a lid covering the rings which lifts up to form a 'splashback'.
  —a mixture of two gas rings and two electric rings.
  Toilet: Main drainage or septic tank? Don't flush disposable
  nappies or anything else down the toilet if you are on a septic
  tank.
  Water: Find the stopcock. Check taps and plugs – they may not
  operate in the way you are used to. Check how to turn on (or
  light) the hot water.
  Windows: Check the method of opening and closing windows
  and shutters.
  Insects: Is an insecticide spray provided? If not, get one locally.
  Equipment: For buying or replacing equipment, see p. 54.
- You will probably have an official agent, but be clear in your
  own mind who to contact in an emergency, even if it is only a
  neighbour in the first place.

WHAT TO SAY

My name is ...	**Mein Name ist ...**
	mine na*h*meh ist ...
I'm staying at ...	**Ich wohne im ...**
	ish v*o*neh im ...
They've cut off ...	**Man hat ... abgestellt**
	man hat ... *u*p-gashtellt
the electricity	**den Strom**
	den shtr*o*me
the gas	**das Gas**
	das g*a*hs
the water	**das Wasser**
	das v*a*sser
Is there ... in the area?	**Gibt es ... in der Nähe?**
	geept es ... in der n*a*y-eh
an electrician	**einen Elektriker**
	*i*nen elek-trik-er
a plumber	**einen Klempner**
	*i*nen klemp-ner
a gas fitter	**einen Installateur**
	*i*nen in-stallah-t*e*r
Where is ...	**Wo ist ...**
	vo ist ...
the fuse box?	**der Sicherungskasten?**
	der z*i*sher-oongs-kasten
the stopcock?	**der Abstellhahn?**
	der *u*p-shtell-hahn
the boiler?	**der Boiler?**
	der b*o*y-ler
the water heater?	**der Warmwasserbereiter?**
	der vahm-v*a*sser-ber*y*ter
Is there ...	**Gibt es hier ...**
	geept es here ...
town gas?	**Stadtgas?**
	sht*a*tt-gahs
bottled gas?	**Flaschengas?**
	fl*a*shen-gahs
a septic tank?	**eine Sickergrube?**
	*i*neh z*i*cker-gr*oo*beh
central heating?	**Zentralheizung?**
	tsentr*a*hl-hy-tsoong
The cooker	**Der Herd**
	der hairt

The hair dryer	**Der Fön**
	der fern
The heating	**Die Heizung**
	dee hy-tsoong
The boiler	**Der Boiler**
	der boy-ler
The iron	**Das Bügeleisen**
	das boogel-izen
The pilot light	**Die Zündflamme**
	dee tsoont-flammeh
The refrigerator	**Der Kühlschrank**
	der kool-shrank
The telephone	**Das Telefon**
	das telefone
The toilet	**Die Toilette**
	dee twa-letteh
The washing machine	**Die Waschmaschine**
	dee vash-machine-eh
The water heater	**Der Warmwasserbereiter**
	der vahm-vasser-beryter
... is not working	**... funktioniert nicht**
	... foonk-tsee-o-neert nisht
Where can I get ...	**Wo kann ich ... bekommen?**
	vo kan ish ... bekommen
an adaptor for this?	**hierfür einen Zwischenstecker**
	here-foor inen tsvishen-shtecker
a bottle of butane gas?	**eine Flasche Butangas**
	ineh flasheh bootahn-gahs
a bottle of propane gas?	**eine Flasche Propangas**
	ineh flasheh bootahn-gahs
a fuse?	**eine Sicherung**
	ineh zisher-oong
an insecticide spray?	**ein Insektenspray**
	ine in-zekten-shpray
a light bulb?	**eine Glühbirne**
	ineh gloo-beerneh
The drain	**Der Abfluss**
	der up-flooss
The sink	**Der Ausguss**
	der ows-gooss
The toilet	**Die Toilette**
	dee twa-letteh
... is blocked	**... ist verstopft**
	.. ist fer-shtopft

The gas is leaking	**Die Gasleitung ist undicht**
	dee gahs-lite-oong ist *oon*-disht
Can you mend it straightaway?	**Können Sie es sofort reparieren?**
	kernnen zee es zofort repareeren
When can you mend it?	**Wann können Sie es reparieren?**
	vann kernnen zee es repareeren
How much do I owe you?	**Wieviel schulde ich Ihnen?**
	vee-feel shooldeh ish *ee*nen
When is the rubbish collected?	**Wann kommt die Müllabfuhr?**
	vann komt dee mooll-up-foor

LIKELY REACTIONS

What's your name?	**Wie ist Ihr Name?**
	vee ist eer nahmeh
What's your address?	**Wie ist Ihre Adresse?**
	vee ist *ee*reh adresseh
There's a shop ...	**Es gibt einen Laden ...**
	es geept *i*nen lahden ...
in town	**in der Stadt**
	in der shtatt
in the village	**im Dorf**
	im dorf
I can't come ...	**Ich kann ... nicht kommen**
	ish kan ... nisht kommen
today	**heute**
	hoy-teh
this week	**diese Woche**
	deezeh vok-eh
I can't come until Monday	**Ich kann erst Montag kommen**
	ish kan erst mone-tahk kommen
I can come ...	**Ich kann ... kommen**
	ish kan ... kommen
on Tuesday	**Dienstag**
	deens-tahk
when you want	**jederzeit**
	yaider-tsyt
Every day	**Jeden Tag**
	yaiden tahk
Every other day	**Jeden zweiten Tag**
	yaiden tsvy-ten tahk
On Wednesdays	**Mittwochs**
[*For days of the week, p. 133*]	mitt-voks

General shopping

The chemist's

**ESSENTIAL
INFORMATION**

- Look for the word
  APOTHEKE (chemist's)
  or this sign:
- There are two kinds of
  chemist in Germany.
  The **APOTHEKE**
  (dispensing chemist's) is
  the place to go for
  prescriptions, medicines
  etc.; toilet and household articles, as well as patent medicines,
  are sold at the **DROGERIE** (chemist's shop).
- Try the chemist *before* going to a doctor: they are usually
  qualified to treat minor injuries.
- Chemists are open during normal business hours, i.e. from
  8.30 a.m. to 12.30 p.m., and from 2.30 to 6.30 p.m. on weekdays. On Saturdays they close at 2.00 p.m.
- Chemists take it in turns to stay open all night and on Sundays.
  If the chemist is shut, a notice on the door will give the
  address of the nearest night (**NACHTDIENST**) and Sunday
  service (**SONNTAGSDIENST**).
- Some toiletries can also be bought at a **PARFÜMERIE** but
  they will be more expensive.
- Finding a chemist, see p. 19.

WHAT TO SAY

I'd like ...	**Ich möchte ...**
	ish m*e*rshteh ...
some Alka Seltzer	**Alka Seltzer**
	alka z*e*ltser
some antiseptic	**ein antiseptisches Mittel**
	ine anti-z*e*ptishes m*i*ttel

I'd like ...	**Ich möchte ...** ish m*e*rshteh ...
some aspirin	**Aspirin** ahs-pee-r*ee*n
some bandages	**Verbandsstoff** fer-b*a*nts-shtoff
some cotton wool	**Watte** v*a*tteh
some eye drops	**Augentropfen** *o*wghen-tropfen
some foot powder	**Fusspuder** f*oo*ss-pooder
some gauze dressing	**Verbandmull** fer-b*a*nt-mooll
some inhalant	**ein Inhaliermittel** ine in-hahl*ee*r-mittel
some insect repellent	**ein Insektenschutzmittel** ine in-z*e*kten-shoots-mittel
some lip salve	**eine Lippensalbe** *i*neh l*i*ppen-zalbeh
some nose drops	**Nasentropfen** n*a*hzen-tropfen
some sticking plaster	**Heftpflaster** heft-pflaster
some throat pastilles	**Halspastillen** h*a*ls-past-ill-en
some Vaseline	**Vaseline** vahzeh-l*ee*neh
I'd like something for ...	**Ich möchte etwas gegen ...** ish m*e*rshteh *e*tvas g*ay*-ghen ...
bites (snakes, dogs)	**Bisswunden** b*i*s-voon-den
burns	**Verbrennungen** fer-bren-*oo*ng-en
chilblains	**Frostbeulen** fr*o*st-boylen
a cold	**Erkältung** er-k*e*lt-oong
constipation	**Verstopfung** fer-sht*o*pf-oong
a cough	**Husten** h*oo*sten

diarrhoea	**Durchfall**
	*doo*rsh-fahl
ear-ache	**Ohrenschmerzen**
	or-en-shmairts-en
flu	**Grippe**
	gr*i*ppeh
scalds	**Verbrühung**
	fer-br*oo*-oong
sore gums	**wundes Zahnfleisch**
	*voo*ndes ts*a*hn-flysh
sprains	**Gelenkverstauchung**
	gal*e*nk-fer-shtow-koong
stings (mosquitos, bees)	**Insektenstiche**
	in-z*e*kten-shtee-sheh
sunburn	**Sonnenbrand**
	z*o*nnen-brant
car (air)/sea sickness	**Reisekrankheit/Seekrankheit**
	r*y*zeh-krank-hite/z*e*h-krank-hite
I need ...	**Ich brauche ...**
	ish br*ow*-keh ...
some baby food	**Babynahrung**
	b*a*by-nah-roong
some contraceptives	**ein Verhütungsmittel**
	ine fer-h*oo*toongs-mittel
some deodorant	**einen Deodorant**
	*i*nen deo-d*o*rant
some disposable nappies	**Papierwindeln**
	pap*ee*r-vin-deln
some handcream	**eine Handcreme**
	*i*neh h*a*nt-craym
some lipstick	**einen Lippenstift**
	*i*nen l*i*ppen-shtift
some make-up remover	**eine Reinigungsmilch**
	*i*neh ry-nee-goongs-milsh
some paper tissues	**Papiertücher**
	pap*ee*r-toosher
some razor blades	**Rasierklingen**
	raz*ee*r-kling-en
some safety pins	**Sicherheitsnadeln**
	z*i*sher-hyts-nahdeln
some sanitary towels	**Monatsbinden**
	m*o*nahts-bin-den

I need...	**Ich brauche**
	ish brow-keh ...
some shaving cream	**eine Rasiercreme**
	*i*neh razeer-craym
some soap	**ein Stück Seife**
	ine shtook zy-feh
some suntan lotion/oil	**Sonnenmilch/öl**
	zonnen-milsh/erl
some talcum powder	**Talkumpuder**
	t*a*l-koom-pooder
some Tampax	**eine Packung Tampax**
	*i*neh p*a*ck-oong t*a*mpax
some toilet paper	**Toilettenpapier**
	twa-letten-papeer
some toothpaste	**eine Tube Zahnpasta**
	*i*neh t*oo*beh tsahn-pasta

[For other essential expressions, see 'Shop talk', p. 57]

Holiday items

ESSENTIAL INFORMATION

- Places to shop at and signs to look for:
  SCHREIBWARENGESCHÄFT (stationery)
  PHOTOGESCHÄFT (films)
  KUNSTGEWERBE (arts and crafts)
  GESCHENKARTIKEL (gifts)
- and the main department stores:
  KARSTADT
  HORTEN
  HERTIE
  KAUHOF

WHAT TO SAY

Where can I buy . . . ?	**Wo kann ich . . . kaufen?**
	vo kan ish . . . kow-fen
I'd like . . .	**Ich möchte . . .**
	ish mershteh
a bag	**eine Tasche**
	ineh tasheh
a beach ball	**einen Strandball**
	inen shtrant-bal
a bucket	**einen Eimer**
	inen imer
an English newspaper	**eine englische Zeitung**
	ineh eng-lisheh tsy-toong
some envelopes	**Briefumschläge**
	breef-oom-shlaig-eh
a guide book	**einen Reiseführer**
	inen ryzeh-foorer
a map (of the area)	**eine Landkarte von dieser Gegend**
	ineh lant-karteh fon deezer gay-ghent
some postcards	**Ansichtskarten**
	un-zishts-karten
a spade	**eine Schaufel**
	ineh sha-oofel
a straw hat	**einen Strohhut**
	inen shtro-hoot
a suitcase	**einen Koffer**
	inen koffer
some sunglasses	**eine Sonnenbrille**
	ineh zonnen-brilleh
a sunshade	**einen Sonnenschirm**
	inen zonnen-sheerm
an umbrella	**einen Regenschirm**
	inen ray-ghen-sheerm
some writing paper	**Schreibpapier**
	shripe-papeer
I'd like . . . [show the camera]	**Ich möchte . . .**
	ish mershteh . . .
a colour film	**einen Farbfilm**
	inen farp-film
a black and white film	**einen Schwarzweiss-Film**
	inen shvarts-vice film

I'd like ... [*show the camera*] **Ich möchte ...**
ish mershteh ...

   for prints   **für Abzüge**
foor *u*p-tsoog-eh

   for slides   **für Dias**
foor dee-ahs

   12 (24/36) exposures   **zwölf (vierundzwanzig/**
                          sechsunddreissig) Aufnahmen
tsverlf (f*ee*r-oont-tsvan-sik/
zex-oont-dry-sik) *o*wf-nahmen

   a standard 8mm film   **einen acht Millimeter Film**
*i*nen ahkt m*i*lli-maiter film

   a super 8 film   **einen Super-Acht-Film**
*i*nen z*oo*per ahkt f*i*lm

   some flash bulbs   **Blitzlichter**
bl*i*ts-lish-ter

This camera is broken   **Diese Kamera ist kaputt**
d*ee*zeh k*a*mera ist kah-p*oo*t

The film is stuck   **Der Film klemmt**
der f*i*lm klemmt

Please can you ...   **Können Sie bitte ...**
k*er*nnen zee b*i*tteh

   develop/print this?   **diesen Film entwickeln/abziehen?**
d*ee*zen film ent-v*i*ckeln/*u*p-tseen

   load the camera?   **den Film einlegen?**
dehn film *i*ne-laygen

[*For other essential expressions, see 'Shop talk', p. 57*]

The tobacconist's

ESSENTIAL INFORMATION

- A tobacconist's is called a **TABAKWAREN** or **ZIGARRENLADEN**.
- Large supermarkets and department stores often have their own 'tobacconist's' on the premises, a kind of stall near the entrance or cash registers.
- The tobacconist's is the only place where you can get tobacco, cigars, pipe utensils, flints etc., whereas cigarettes can be bought at a variety of places:
  at the **KIOSK**
  at most foodstores
  from the cigarette machine round the corner
  inside a café, bar or pub etc.
- To ask if there is a tobacconist's near by, see p. 19.

WHAT TO SAY

A packet of cigarettes . . .	**Eine Schachtel Zigaretten . . .** *i*neh sh*a*ktel tsee-garetten . . .
with filters	**mit Filter** mit f*i*lter
without filters	**ohne Filter** *o*-neh f*i*lter
king size	**extra lang** *e*xtrah l*a*ng
menthol	**mit Menthol** mit men-t*o*le
Those up there . . .	**Die da oben . . .** dee dah *o*-ben . . .
on the right	**rechts** reshts
on the left	**links** links
These [*point*]	**Diese hier** d*ee*zeh here
Cigarettes, please	**Zigaretten, bitte** tsee-gar*e*tten b*i*tteh

100, 200, 300	**einhundert, zweihundert, dreihundert**
	*i*ne-hoondert tsvy-hoondert dry-hoondert
Two packets	**Zwei Schachteln**
	tsvy sh*a*kteln
Have you got ...	**Haben Sie ...**
	h*a*hben zee
English cigarettes?	**englische Zigaretten?**
	eng-lisheh tsee-gar*e*tten
American cigarettes?	**amerikanische Zigaretten?**
	ameri-k*a*h-nisheh tsee-gar*e*tten
English pipe tobacco?	**englischen Pfeifentabak?**
	eng-lishen pf*y*fen-tabak
American pipe tobacco?	**amerikanischen Pfeifentabak?**
	ameri-k*a*h-nishen pf*y*fen-tabak
rolling tobacco?	**Zigarettentabak?**
	tsee-gar*e*tten-tabak
A packet of pipe tobacco	**Eine Packung Pfeifentabak**
	*i*neh p*a*ck-oong pf*y*fen-tabak
That one down there ...	**Den da unten ...**
	dehn dah *oo*nten ...
on the right	**rechts**
	reshts
on the left	**links**
	links
This one [*point*]	**Diesen hier**
	d*ee*zen here
A cigar, please	**Eine Zigarre, bitte**
	*i*neh tsee-g*a*rreh b*i*tteh
That one [*point*]	**Die da**
	d*ee* dah
Some cigars, please	**Zigarren, bitte**
	tsee-g*a*rren b*i*tteh
Those [*point*]	**Die da**
	d*ee* dah
A box of matches	**Eine Schachtel Streichhölzer**
	*i*neh sh*a*ktel shtrysh-h*e*rltser
A packet of pipe-cleaners	**Eine Packung Pfeifenreiniger**
	*i*neh p*a*ck-oong pf*y*fen-ry-neeg-er

A packet of flints	**Eine Packung Feuersteine**
[show lighter]	*ineh* p**a**ck-oong f**o**y-er-shtine-eh
Lighter fuel	**Feuerzeugbenzin**
	f**o**y-er-tsoyk-bentseen
Lighter gas, please	**Feuerzeuggass, bitte**
	f**o**y-er-tsoyk-gahs b**i**tteh

[*For other essential expressions, see 'Shop talk', p. 57*]

Buying clothes

ESSENTIAL INFORMATION

- Look for:
  DAMENBEKLEIDUNG (women's clothes)
  HERRENBEKLEIDUNG (men's clothes)
  SCHUHGESCHÄFT (shoe shop)
- Don't buy without being measured first or without trying things on.
- Don't rely on conversion charts of clothing sizes (see p. 144).
- If you are buying for someone else, take their measurements with you.
- All major department stores [*see p. 44*] sell clothes and shoes.

WHAT TO SAY

I'd like ...	**Ich möchte ...**
	ish mershteh ...
an anorak	**einen Anorak**
	inen **a**h-norak
a belt	**einen Gürtel**
	inen g**oo**r-tel
a bikini	**einen Bikini**
	inen bik**i**ni
a bra	**einen Büstenhalter/BH**
	inen b**oo**sten-halter/beh-h**a**h

I'd like . . .	**Ich möchte . . .**
	ish m*e*rshteh . . .
a cap (swimming)	**eine Badekappe**
	*i*neh b*a*hdeh-kappeh
(skiing)	**eine Skimütze**
	*i*neh sh*ee*-mootseh
a cardigan	**eine Wolljacke**
	*i*neh v*o*ll-yackeh
a coat	**einen Mantel**
	*i*nen m*a*ntel
a dress	**ein Kleid**
	ine kl*i*te
a hat	**einen Hut**
	*i*nen hoot
a jacket	**eine Jacke**
	*i*neh y*a*h-keh
a jumper	**einen Pullover**
	*i*nen pull-*o*ver
a nightdress	**ein Nachthemd**
	ine n*a*kt-hemt
a pullover	**einen Pullover**
	*i*nen pull-*o*ver
some pyjamas	**einen Schlafanzug**
	*i*nen shl*a*hf-un-tsook
a raincoat	**einen Regenmantel**
	*i*nen r*a*y-ghen-mantel
a shirt (women)	**eine Bluse**
	*i*neh bl*oo*zeh
a shirt (men)	**ein Oberhemd**
	ine *o*-ber-hemt
a skirt	**einen Rock**
	*i*nen rock
a suit (women)	**ein Kostüm**
	ine kost-*oo*m
a suit (men)	**einen Anzug**
	*i*nen *u*n-tsook
a swimsuit	**einen Badeanzug**
	*i*nen b*a*hdeh-un-tsook
some tights	**eine Strumpfhose**
	*i*neh shtr*oo*mpf-hozeh
some trousers	**eine Hose**
	*i*neh h*o*zeh

a T-shirt	**ein T-Shirt**
	ine t*ee*-shirt
I'd like a pair of ...	**Ich möchte ein Paar ...**
	ish m*e*rshteh ine p*a*r ...
briefs (women)	**Damenschlüpfer**
	d*a*hmen-shloopfer
gloves	**Handschuhe**
	h*a*nt-shoo-eh
jeans	**Jeans**
	jeans
shorts	**Shorts**
	shorts
(short/long) socks	**(Kurze/lange) Socken**
	(k*oo*r-tseh/l*a*ngeh) z*o*cken
stockings	**Strümpfe**
	shtr*oo*m-feh
underpants (men)	**Herrenunterhosen**
	h*e*rren-oonter-hozen
I'd like a pair of ...	**Ich möchte ein Paar ...**
	ish m*e*rshteh ine p*a*r
shoes	**Schuhe**
	sh*oo*-eh
canvas shoes	**Tennisschuhe**
	tennis-sh*oo*-eh
sandals	**Sandalen**
	zand*a*hlen
beach shoes	**Strandsandalen**
	shtr*a*nt-zand*a*hlen
smart shoes	**elegante Schuhe**
	ele-g*a*nteh sh*oo*eh
boots	**Stiefel**
	sht*ee*-fel
moccasins	**Mokassins**
	mok*a*ssins
My size is ...	**Ich habe Grösse ...**
	ish h*a*hbeh gr*e*rsseh ...

[*For numbers, see p. 129*]

Can you measure me, please?	**Können Sie bitte meine Masse nehmen?**
	k*e*rnnen zee b*i*tteh m*i*neh m*a*hsseh nay-men

Can I try it on?	**Kann ich es anprobieren?**
	kan ish es *un*-pro-beeren
It's for a present	**Es soll ein Geschenk sein**
	es zoll ine gash*e*nk zine
These are the measurements	**Hier sind die Masse**
[*show written*]	here zint dee m*a*hsseh
bust	**Oberweite**
	o-ber-vy-teh
chest	**Brustumfang**
	br*oo*st-oom-fang
collar	**Kragenweite**
	kr*a*h-ghen-vy-teh
hip	**Hüftumfang**
	h*oo*ft-oom-fang
leg	**Beinlänge**
	b*i*ne-leng-eh
waist	**Taillenweite**
	t*a*l-yen-vy-teh
Have you got something ...	**Haben Sie etwas ...**
	h*a*hben zee *e*tvas ...
in black?	**in schwarz?**
	in shv*a*rts
in white?	**in weiss?**
	in v*i*ce
in grey?	**in grau?**
	in gr*a*-oo
in blue?	**in blau?**
	in bl*a*-oo
in brown?	**in braun?**
	in brown
in pink?	**in rosa?**
	in r*o*za
in green?	**in grün?**
	in gr*oo*n
in red?	**in rot?**
	in r*o*te
in yellow?	**in gelb?**
	in gh*e*lp
in this colour? [*point*]	**in dieser Farbe?**
	in d*ee*zer farbeh
in cotton?	**in Baumwolle?**
	in b*o*wm-volleh

in denim?	**in Jeansstoff?**
	in jeans-shtoff
in leather?	**in Leder?**
	in lay-der
in nylon?	**in Nylon?**
	in nylon
in suede?	**in Wildleder?**
	in vilt-lay-der
in wool?	**in Wolle?**
	in volleh
in this material? *[point]*	**in diesem Material?**
	in deezem materi-ahl

[For other essential expressions, see 'Shop talk', p. 57]

Replacing equipment

ESSENTIAL INFORMATION

- Look for these shops and signs:
  EISENWARENHANDLUNG (hardware)
  HAUSHALTSWAREN (household goods)
  ELEKTROGESCHÄFT (electrical goods)
  DROGERIE (household cleaning materials)
- In a supermarket, look for this display:
  HAUSHALTSARTIKEL
- To ask the way to the shop, see p. 19.
- At a campsite try their shop first.

WHAT TO SAY

Have you got . . .

Haben Sie . . .
hahben zee . . .

an adaptor? [*show appliance*]

einen Zwischenstecker?
inen tsvishen-shtecker

a bottle of butane gas?

eine Flasche Butangas?
ineh flasheh bootahn-gahs

a bottle of propane gas?

eine Flasche Propangas?
ineh flasheh pro-pahn-gahs

a bottle opener?

einen Flaschenöffner?
inen flashen-erffner

a corkscrew?

einen Korkenzieher?
inen korken-tsee-er

any disinfectant?

ein Desinfektionsmittel?
ine des-infek-tsee-ons-mittel

any disposable cups?

Pappbecher?
pap-besher

any disposable plates?

Pappteller?
pap-teller

a drying up cloth?

ein Geschirrtuch?
ine gasheer-took

any forks?

Gabeln?
gah-beln

a fuse? [*show old one*]

eine Sicherung?
ineh zisher-oong

an insecticide spray?	**ein Insektenspray?** ine in-zekten-shpray
a paper kitchen roll?	**eine Rolle Küchenpapier?** *i*neh rolleh koo-shen-papeer
any knives?	**Messer?** messer
a light bulb [*show old one*]	**eine Glühbirné?** *i*neh gloo-beer-neh
a plastic bucket?	**einen Plastikeimer?** *i*nen plastik-*i*mer
a plastic can?	**einen Plastikkanister?** *i*nen plastik-kan*i*ster
a scouring pad?	**einen Topfkratzer?** *i*nen topf-kratser
a spanner?	**einen Schraubenschlüssel?** *i*nen shrowben-shloossel
a sponge?	**einen Schwamm?** *i*nen shvamm
any string?	**Bindfaden?** b*i*nt-fahden
any tent pegs?	**Heringe fürs Zelt?** hering-eh foors tselt
a tin opener?	**einen Dosenöffner?** *i*nen doze-en-erffner
a torch?	**eine Taschenlampe?** *i*neh tashen-lampeh
any torch batteries?	**Taschenlampenbatterien?** tashen-lampen-batter-*ee*-en
a universal plug (for the sink)?	**einen Stöpsel (für das Spülbecken)?** *i*nen shterp-zel foor das shpool-becken
a washing line?	**eine Wäscheleine?** *i*neh vesheh-line-eh
any washing powder?	**Waschpulver?** vash-poolver
a washing-up brush?	**eine Spülbürste?** *i*neh shpool-boorsteh
any washing-up liquid?	**ein Spülmittel?** ine shpool-mittel

[*For other essential expressions, see 'Shop talk', p. 57*]

Shop talk

ESSENTIAL INFORMATION

- Know your coins and notes.
  German coins: see illustration.
  German notes: 5, 10, 20, 50, 100 Deutschmark
  Austrian coins: 1, 2, 5, 10, 20, 50 Groschen; 1, 5, 10 Schilling
  Austrian notes: 20, 50, 100, 500 Schilling
  Swiss coins: 5, 10, 20, 50 Rappen; 1, 2, 5 Franken
  Swiss notes: 10, 20, 50, 100 Franken
- Know how to say the important weights and measures: note that though Germany is metric, people still use the word **Pfund** (pound).

50 grams	**fünfzig Gramm**
	*fo*onf-tsik gr*a*mm
100 grams	**einhundert Gramm**
	*i*ne-hoondert gr*a*mm
200 grams	**zweihundert Gramm**
	tsv*y*-hoondert gr*a*mm
½ lb (250 grams)	**ein halbes Pfund**
	*i*ne h*a*lbes pfoont
1 lb	**ein Pfund**
	*i*ne pfoont
1 kilo	**ein Kilo**
	*i*ne k*i*lo
2 kilos	**zwei Kilo**
	tsv*y* k*i*lo
½ litre	**einen halben Liter**
	*i*nen h*a*lben l*i*tre
1 litre	**einen Liter**
	*i*nen l*i*tre
2 litres	**zwei Liter**
[*For numbers, see p. 129*]	tsv*y* l*i*tre

- In small shops don't be surprised if customers, as well as the shop asistant, say 'hello' and 'good-bye' to you.

CUSTOMER

Hello	**Guten Tag** goo-ten tahk
Hello (Austria)	**Grüss Gott** grooss got
Good morning	**Guten Morgen** goo-ten morgen
Good afternoon	**Guten Tag** goo-ten tahk
Good-bye	**Auf Wiedersehn** owf veeder-zain
I'm just looking	**Ich sehe mich nur um** ish zay-eh mish noor oom
Excuse me	**Entschuldigen Sie** ent-shool-dig-en zee
How much is this/that?	**Wieviel kostet dies/das?** vee-feel kostet dees/das
What is that? /What are those?	**Was ist das?** vas ist das
Is there a discount?	**Gibt es einen Rabatt?** geept es inen rah- batt
I'd like that, please	**Ich möchte das da, bitte** ish mershteh das dah bitteh
Not that	**Nicht das** nisht das
Like that	**Wie das da** vee das dah
That's enough, thank you	**Das ist genug, danke** das ist ganook dankeh
More please	**Mehr, bitte** mair bitteh
Less than that	**Etwas weniger** etvas vay-neeg-er
That's fine	**Das ist gut so** das ist goot zo
OK	**Gut** goot
I won't take it, thank you	**Ich nehme es nicht, danke** ish nay-meh es nisht dankeh
It's not right	**Es ist nicht das Richtige** es ist nisht das rish-teeg-eh

Thank you very much	**Vielen Dank**
	fee-len dank
Have you got something ...	**Haben Sie etwas ...**
	hahben zee etvas
better?	**Besseres?**
	besser-es
cheaper?	**Billigeres?**
	billig-er-es
different?	**anderes?**
	ander-es
larger?	**Grösseres?**
	grersser-es
smaller?	**Kleineres?**
	kliner-es
At what time do you ...	**Um wieviel Uhr ...**
	oom vee-feel oor ...
open?	**öffnen Sie?**
	erffnen zee
close?	**schliessen Sie?**
	shleessen zee
Can I have a bag, please?	**Kann ich bitte eine Tragetasche haben?**
	kan ish bitteh ineh trahg-eh-tasheh hahben
Can I have a receipt?	**Kann ich eine Quittung haben?**
	kan ish ineh kvitt-oong hahben
Do you take ...	**Nehmen Sie ...**
	nay-men zee ...
English/American money?	**englisches/amerikanisches Geld?**
	eng-lishes/ameri-kah-nishes ghelt
travellers' cheques?	**Reiseschecks?**
	ryzeh-shecks
credit cards?	**Kreditkarten?**
	kredeet-karten
I'd like ...	**Ich möchte ...**
	ish mershteh ...
one like that	**eins davon**
	ines dah-fon
two like that	**zwei davon**
	tsvy dah-fon

SHOP ASSISTANT

Can I help you?	**Kann ich Ihnen behilflich sein?**
	kan ish _ee_nen beh_i_lf-lish zine
What would you like?.	**Was darf es sein**
	vas darf es zine
Will that be all?.	**Kommt noch etwas dazu?**
	komt nok _e_tvas dah-tsoo
Is that all?	**Ist das alles?**
	ist das _a_lles
Anything else?	**Sonst noch etwas?**
	_zo_nst nok _e_tvas
Would you like it wrapped?	**Soll ich es einwickeln?**
	zoll ish es _i_ne-vickeln
Sorry, none left	**Leider ausverkauft**
	_li_der _o_ws-fer-kowft
I haven't got any	**Wir haben keine**
	veer h_a_hben k_i_neh
I haven't got any more	**Wir haben keine mehr**
	veer h_a_hben k_i_neh mair
How many do you want?	**Wieviele möchten Sie?**
	vee-feeleh m_e_rshten zee
How much do you want?	**Wieviel möchten Sie?**
	vee-feel m_e_rshten zee
Is that enough?	**Ist das genug?**
	ist das gan_oo_k

Shopping for food

Bread

ESSENTIAL INFORMATION

- Finding a baker's, see p. 19.
- Key words to look for:
  BÄCKEREI (baker's)
  BÄCKER (baker)
  BROT (bread)
- Supermarkets of any size and general stores nearly always sell bread.
- Bakers are open from 7.30 a.m. to 12.30 p.m. and from 2.30 to 6.30 p.m. on weekdays. On Saturdays they close at lunchtime. Many bakers will open on Sunday mornings from 10 a.m. to noon and close one afternoon during the week, usually on Wednesdays.

WHAT TO SAY

Some bread, please	**Brot, bitte** brote bitteh
A loaf (like that)	**Ein Brot (wie das da)** ine brote (vee das dah)
A large one	**Ein grosses** ine grosses
A small one	**Ein kleines** ine kline-es
A bread roll	**Ein Brötchen** ine brert-shen
A bread roll (Bavaria, Austria)	**Eine Semmel** ineh zemmel
A crescent roll	**Ein Hörnchen** ine hern-shen
Bread	**Brot** brote
Sliced bread	**Geschnittenes Brot** ga-shnitten-es brote

White bread	**Weissbrot** vice-brote
Rye bread	**Graubrot** gra-oo-brote
(Black) rye bread	**Schwarzbrot** shvarts-brote
Wholemeal bread	**Vollkornbrot** foll-korn-brote
Two loaves	**Zwei Brote** tsvy brote-eh
Four bread rolls	**Vier Brötchen** feer brert-shen
Four crescent rolls	**Vier Hörnchen** feer hern-shen

[*For other essential expressions, see 'Shop talk', p. 57*]

Cakes

ESSENTIAL INFORMATION

- Key words to look for:
  BÄCKEREI (bread and cake shop)
  KONDITOREI (cake shop, often with a tea-room in the back)
- To find a cake shop, see p. 19.
- **CAFÉ** or **KAFFEEHAUS** in Austria: a place to buy cakes and have a drink at a table, usually in the afternoon. See also p. 80, 'Ordering a drink'.

WHAT TO SAY

The type of cakes you find in the shops varies slightly from region to region but the following are some of the most common.

der Berliner der ber-*lee*ner	jam filled doughnut
der Florentiner der flor-en-*tee*ner	almond flakes on a thin cake and chocolate base

die Schwarzwälder Kirschtorte	Black Forest cake
dee shvarts-velder keersh-torteh	
die Obsttorte	fruit on a sponge base with glazing over
dee obst-torteh	
der Apfelstrudel	flaky pastry filled with apple, nuts, and raisins
der apfel-shtroodel	
der Mohrenkopf	ball-shaped pastry filled with pudding, covered with chocolate
der moren-kopf	
der Käsekuchen	cheesecake
der kaizeh-kooken	
die Sachertorte	rich Viennese chocolate cake with jam
dee zahker-torteh	
der Sandkuchen	Madeira cake
der zant-kooken	
die Sahnetorte	cream cake
dee zah-neh-torteh	
der Bienenstich	cream cake sprinkled with flaky almonds and honey
der beenen-shtish	

You usually buy individual pastries by number:

Two doughnuts, please	**Zwei Berliner, bitte**
	tsvy ber-leener bitteh

You buy large cakes by the slice:

One slice of fruit tart	**Ein Stück Obsttorte**
	ine shtook obst-torteh
Two slices of Madeira cake	**Zwei Stück Sandkuchen**
	tsvy shtook zant-kooken

You may also want to say:

With whipped cream, please	**Mit Sahne, bitte**
	mit zah-neh bitteh

[For other essential expressions, see 'Shop talk', p. 57]

Ice-cream and sweets

ESSENTIAL INFORMATION

- Key words to look for:
  EIS (ice-cream)
  EISDIELE (ice-cream parlour)
  EISCAFÉ (ice-cream parlour/tea room)
  SÜSSWARENLADEN (sweet shop)
  KONDITOREI (cake shop)
- Best known ice-cream brand names:
  LANGNESE   SCHÖLLER
  DR OETKER   JOPA
- Pre-packed sweets are available in general stores and super-markets.

WHAT TO SAY

A ... ice, please...

	Ein ...-Eis, bitte
	ine ... ice bitteh
strawberry	**Erdbeer**
	airt-bear
chocolate	**Schokoladen**
	shoko-lahden
vanilla	**Vanille**
	vanilyeh
lemon	**Zitronen**
	tsee-tronen
caramel	**Karamel**
	kara-mel
raspberry	**Himbeer**
	him-bear

At the table

A single portion	**Eine kleine Portion**
	ineh kly-neh por-tsee-on
Two single portions	**Zwei kleine Portionen**
	tsvy kly-neh por-tsee-onen
A double portion	**Eine grosse Portion**
	ineh grosseh por-tsee-on

Two double portions	**Zwei grosse Portionen** tsvy grosseh por-tsee-*o*nen
A mixed ice ...	**Ein gemischtes Eis ...** ine ga-mishtes ice ...
with/without whipped cream	**mit/ohne Sahne** mit/*o*hneh zahneh

Over the counter

A cone ...	**Ein Hörnchen ...** ine hern-shen ...
A tub ...	**Einen Becher ...** inen besher ...
with two scoops	**mit zwei Kugeln** mit tsvy k*oo*g-eln
with three scoops	**mit drei Kugeln** mit dry k*oo*g-eln
(60 Pfennig's) worth of ice-cream	**Ein Eis zu (sechzig)** ine ice tsoo (zek-tsig)
A packet of ...	**Eine Packung ...** ineh pack-oong ...
100 grams of ...	**Hundert Gramm ...** h*oo*ndert gramm ...
200 grams of ...	**Zweihundert Gramm ...** tsvy-h*oo*ndert gramm ...
sweets	**Bonbons** bong-bongs
toffees	**Karamelbonbons** karamel-bong-bongs
chocolates	**Pralinen** pra-l*ee*nen
mints	**Pfefferminzbonbons** pfeffer-mints-bong-bongs
A lollipop	**Einen Dauerlutscher** inen d*o*wer-lootsher

[*For other essential expressions, see 'Shop talk', p. 57*]

In the supermarket

ESSENTIAL INFORMATION

- The place to ask for: [*see p. 19*]
  EIN SUPERMARKT
  EIN SELBSTBEDIENUNGSLADEN (corner self-service)
  EIN LEBENSMITTELGESCHÄFT (general food store)
- Key instructions on signs in the shop:
  EINGANG (entrance)
  KEIN EINGANG (no entry)
  AUSGANG (exit)
  KEIN AUSGANG (no exit)
  KASSE (check-out, cash desk)
  SCHNELLKASSE (check-out for up to five items)
  IM ANGEBOT (on offer)
  SONDERANGEBOT (special offer)
  SELBSTBEDIENUNG (self-service)
- Large supermarkets are open all day from 8.00 a.m. to 6.30 p.m. The smaller corner shops usually close at lunchtime, from 12.30 to 2.30 p.m.
- For non-food items, see 'Replacing equipment', p.54.
- No need to say anything in a supermarket, but ask if you can't see what you want.

WHAT TO SAY

Excuse me, please	**Entschuldigen Sie, bitte**
	ent-sh*oo*l-dig-en zee b*i*tteh
Where is ...	**Wo ist ...**
	vo ist ...
the bread?	**das Brot?**
	das br*o*te
the butter?	**die Butter?**
	dee b*oo*tter
the cheese?	**der Käse?**
	der k*ay*-zeh
the chocolate?	**die Schokolade?**
	dee shoko-l*ah*deh

the coffee?	**der Kaffee?**
	der k*a*ffeh
the cooking oil?	**das Speiseöl?**
	das shp*i*zeh-erl
the fresh fish section?	**die Fischabteilung?**
	dee f*i*sh-abt*i*le-oong
the fruit?	**das Obst?**
	das *o*bst
the jam?	**die Marmelade?**
	dee marmeh-l*a*hdeh
the meat?	**das Fleisch?**
	das fl*y*sh
the milk?	**die Milch?**
	dee m*i*lsh
the mineral water	**das Mineralwasser?**
	das miner*a*hl-vasser
the salt?	**das Salz?**
	das z*a*lts
the sugar?	**der Zucker?**
	der ts*oo*cker
the tea?	**der Tee?**
	der t*a*y
the vegetable section?	**die Gemüseabteilung?**
	dee gam*oo*zeh-abt*i*loong
the vinegar?	**der Essig?**
	der *e*ssik
the wine?	**der Wein?**
	der v*i*ne
the yoghurt?	**der Joghurt?**
	der y*o*g-oort
Where are ...	**Wo sind ...**
	v*o* zint ...
the biscuits?	**die Kekse?**
	dee c*a*ke-seh
the crisps?	**die Kartoffelchips?**
	dee kar-t*o*ffel-ships
the eggs?	**die Eier?**
	dee *eye*-er
the frozen foods?	**die Tiefkühlwaren?**
	dee t*ee*f-kool-vahren
the fruit juices?	**die Fruchtsäfte?**
	dee fr*oo*kt-zefteh

Where are . . .	**Wo sind . . .**
	vo zint . . .
the pastas?	**die Teigwaren?**
	dee tike-vahren
the soft drinks?	**die alkoholfreien Getränke?**
	dee alkohol-fry-en gatrenkeh
the sweets?	**die Süssigkeiten?**
	dee zoo-sick-kiten
the tinned vegetables?	**die Gemüsekonserven?**
	dee ga-moozeh-kon-zairven
the tinned foods?	**die Konserven?**
	dee kon-zairven

[For other essential expressions, see 'Shop talk', p. 57]

Picnic food

ESSENTIAL INFORMATION

- Key words to look for:
  DELIKATESSENGESCHÄFT
  FEINKOSTGESCHÄFT ⎱ (delicatessen)
  METZGEREI
  SCHLACHTEREI ⎰ (butcher's)
- Weight guide:
  4-6 oz/150 g of prepared salad per two people, if eaten as a starter to a substantial meal.
  3-4 oz/100 g of prepared salad per person, if to be eaten as the main part of a picnic-type meal.

WHAT TO SAY

One slice of . . .	**Eine Scheibe . . .**
	ineh shy-beh . . .
Two slices of . . .	**Zwei Scheiben . . .**
	tsvy shy-ben . . .
roast beef	**Rostbraten**
	rost-brahten

tongue sausage	**Zungenwurst**
	tsoongen-voorst
Saveloy sausage	**Zervelatwurst**
	zervelaht-voorst
raw cured ham	**rohen Schinken**
	ro-en shinken
cooked ham	**gekochten Schinken**
	gakokten shinken
garlic sausage	**Knoblauchwurst**
	knop-lowk-voorst
salami	**Salami**
	zalah-mi
100 grams of ...	**Hundert Gramm ...**
	hoondert gramm ...
150 grams of ...	**Hundertfünfzig Gramm ...**
	hoondert-foonf-tsick gram ...
200 grams of ...	**Zweihundert Gramm ...**
	tsvy-hoondert gram ...
300 grams of ...	**Dreihundert Gramm ...**
	dry-hoondert gram ...
herring salad	**Heringsalat**
	hering-zalaht
egg and mayonnaise salad	**Eiersalat**
	eye-er-zalaht
chicken salad	**Geflügelsalat**
	gafloog-el-zalaht
tomato salad	**Tomatensalat**
	tomahten-zalaht
potato salad	**Kartoffelsalat**
	kartoffel-zalaht

You might also like to try some of these:

eine Pizza	a pizza
ineh pizza	
ein Stück Gänseleberpastete	some goose liver pâté
ine shtook	
ghen-zeh-laber-pastaiteh	
ein Stück Fleischwurst	some luncheon sausage
ine shtook flysh-voorst	
einen Matjeshering	white salted herring
inen mat-yes-hering	

eine Frikadelle	a spicy thick hamburger
*i*neh frikah-d*e*lleh	(often eaten cold)
einen Räucheraal	a smoked eel
*i*nen r*o*y-sher-ahl	
ein Paar Frankfurter	two Frankfurter sausages
ine par fr*a*nk-foorter	
eine Weisswurst	a Bavarian sausage
*i*neh v*i*ce-voorst	
eine Thüringer Bratwurst	a spicy sausage from Thuringia
*i*neh t*oo*ring-er br*a*ht-voorst	
einen Elsässer Wurstsalat	shredded meat and cheese salad
*i*nen *e*l-zesser voorst-zalaht	
ein Stück Leberkäse	some meatloaf
ine shtook l*a*ber-kay-zeh	
eine Wurstpastete	a sausage roll
*i*neh v*o*orst-past*ai*teh	
eine Königin-Pastete	a vol-au-vent
*i*neh k*e*rneeg-in past*ai*teh	
eine Geflügelpastete	a chicken vol-au-vent
*i*neh gafl*oo*g-el-past*ai*teh	
einen Kräuterquark	soft cream cheese with herbs
*i*nen kr*o*yter-kwark	
Tilsiter	mild cheese
t*i*l-zit-er	
Kümmelkäse	cheese with caraway seeds
k*o*ommel-kaizeh	
einen Harzer Roller	sharp roll-shaped cheese
*i*nen h*a*rtser r*o*ller	
Emmentaler	Swiss cheese
*e*mmen-tahler	
Gouda	Dutch cheese
g*o*wdah	
Camembert/Brie	Camembert/Brie
c*a*men-bair/br*ee*	

[*For other essential expressions, see 'Shop talk', p. 57*]

Fruit and vegetables

ESSENTIAL INFORMATION

- Key words to look for:
  OBST (fruit)
  GEMÜSE (vegetables)
  OBST- UND GEMÜSEHÄNDLER (greengrocer)
- If possible, buy fruit and vegetables in the market where they
  are cheaper and fresher than in the shops.
- Weight guide:
  1 kilo of potatoes is sufficient for six people for one meal.

WHAT TO SAY

1lb (½ kilo) of ...	**Ein Pfund (ein halbes Kilo)** ...
	*i*ne pfoont (*i*ne h*a*lbes k*i*lo) ...
1 kilo of ...	**Ein Kilo** ...
	*i*ne k*i*lo ...
2 kilos of ...	**Zwei Kilo** ...
	tsv*y* k*i*lo ...
apples	**Äpfel**
	*e*pfel
bananas	**Bananen**
	ban*a*h-nen
cherries	**Kirschen**
	k*ee*r-shen
grapes	**Weintrauben**
	v*i*ne-tra-ooben
oranges	**Apfelsinen**
	apfel-z*ee*nen
pears	**Birnen**
	b*ee*r-nen
peaches	**Pfirsiche**
	pf*ee*r-zisheh
plums	**Pflaumen**
	pfla-*oo*men
strawberries	**Erdbeeren**
	*ai*rd-bairen
A pineapple, please	**Eine Ananas, bitte**
	*i*neh ah-nanas b*i*tteh

A grapefruit	**Eine Pampelmuse**
	*i*neh pampel-m*oo*zeh
A melon	**Eine Melone**
	*i*neh melone-eh
A water melon	**Eine Wassermelone**
	*i*neh v*a*sser-melone-eh
½lb of …	**Ein halbes Pfund …**
	*i*ne h*a*lbes pfoont
1lb of …	**Ein Pfund …**
	*i*ne pfoont …
1 kilo of …	**Ein Kilo …**
	*i*ne k*i*lo …
3lbs of …	**Drei Pfund …**
	dr*y* pfoont …
2 kilos of …	**Zwei Kilo …**
	tsv*y* k*i*lo …
artichokes	**Artischocken**
	arti-sh*o*ken
aubergines	**Auberginen**
	ober-g*ee*nen
avocado pears	**Avokados**
	ahvo-k*a*hdos
carrots	**Karotten**
	kar*o*tten
courgettes	**Zucchini**
	tsoo-k*i*ni
green beans	**grüne Bohnen**
	gr*oo*neh b*o*ne-en
leeks	**Lauch/Porree**
	lowk/p*o*r-ray
mushrooms	**Pilze**
	p*i*l-tseh
onions	**Zwiebeln**
	tsv*ee*-beln
peas	**Erbsen**
	*ai*rpsen
potatoes	**Kartoffeln**
	kar-t*o*ffeln
red cabbage	**Rotkohl**
	r*o*te-kole
spinach	**Spinat**
	shpee-n*a*ht
tomatoes	**Tomaten**
	tom*a*hten

A bunch of ...	Ein Bund ... *i*ne boont ...
parsley	**Petersilie** pater-*zeel*-yeh
radishes	**Radieschen** rah-*dees*-shen
shallots	**Schalotten** shah-*lotten*
A head of garlic	**Knoblauch** k*nope*-la-ook
A lettuce	**Einen Kopfsalat** *i*nen k*opf*-zalaht
A cauliflower	**Einen Blumenkohl** *i*nen bl*oo*men-kole
A cabbage	**Einen Weisskohl** *i*nen *vice*-kole
A cucumber	**Eine Salatgurke** *i*neh zal*aht*-goorkeh
Like that, please	**So eine, bitte** zo *i*neh b*i*tteh

Here are some fruit and vegetables which may not be familiar:

Zwetschgen tsv*etsh*-gen	type of plum used for plum tart
Sauerkirsche zow-er-*keer*sheh	small sour-tasting variety of cherry
Reneklode reneh-kl*o*deh	small yellow plum
Mandarine mandah-*ree*neh	mandarin orange
Klementine klemen-*tee*neh	pipless, small tangerine
Kohlrabi kole-r*ah*bee	vegetable similar to turnip in shape and taste
Fenchel fenshel	fennel, crunchy vegetable with aniseed flavour
Wirsingkohl veer-*zing*-kole	Savoy, variety of cabbage

[*For other essential expressions, see 'Shop talk', p. 57*]

Beef Rind

1 Hals
2 Zungenstück Zungengrat
3 Hohe Rippe
4 Filet (Lende)
5 Hüfte
6 Schwanzstück
7 Stich
8 Schulter
9 Querrippe (Zwerchrippe)
10 Blume (Rose)
11 Brust
12 Bauch (Nabel)
13 Beinfleisch

Veal Kalb

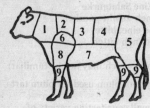

1 Hals
2 Nacken
3 Kotelett
4 Nierenbraten
5 Keule (Schlegel)
6 Blatt
7 Brust
8 Schulter
9 Haxe

Pork Schwein

1 Keule
2 Rücken
3 Nacken (Kamm)
4 Bauch
5 Schulter (Vorderschinken)
6 Eisbein

Mutton Hammel

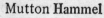

1 Keule
2 Rücken
3 Hals
4 Brust
5 Schulter

Meat

ESSENTIAL INFORMATION

- Key words to look for:

METZGEREI		METZGER	
FLEISCHEREI	(butcher's)	FLEISCHER	(butcher)
SCHLACHTEREI		SCHLACHTER	

- Weight guide: 4-6 oz/125-200 g of meat per person for one meal.
- The diagrams opposite are to help you make sense of labels on counters and supermarket displays, and decide which cut or joint to have. Translations do not help, and you don't need to say the German word involved.
- You will find that lamb and especially mutton are less popular in Germany. The butcher's display will tell you what's available.

WHAT TO SAY

For a joint, choose the type of meat and then say how many people it is for:

Some beef, please	**Rindfleisch, bitte**
	rint-flysh bitteh
Some lamb	**Lamm**
	lamm
Some mutton	**Hammelfleisch**
	hammel-flysh
Some pork	**Schweinefleisch**
	shvine-eh-flysh
Some veal	**Kalbfleisch**
	kalp-flysh
A joint ...	**Einen Braten ...**
	inen brahten ...
for two people	**für zwei Personen**
	foor tsvy per-zonen
for four people	**für vier Personen**
	foor feer per-zonen

For steak, liver or kidneys, do as above:

Some steak, please	**Steak, bitte** steak bitte
Some liver	**Leber** laber
Some kidneys	**Nieren** neeren
Some sausages	**Würstchen** voorst-shen
Some minced meat	**Hackfleisch** hack-flysh
for three people	**für drei Personen** foor dry per-zonen
for five people	**für fünf Personen** foor foonf per-zonen

For chops, do it this way:

Two veal scallops, please	**Zwei Kalbsschnitzel, bitte** tsvy kalps-shnitsel bitteh
Three pork chops	**Drei Schweinekoteletts** dry shvine-eh-kotlets
Five lamb chops	**Fünf Lammkoteletts** foonf lamm-kotlets

You may also want:

A chicken	**Ein Huhn** ine hoon
A tongue	**Eine Zunge** ineh tsoong-eh

Other essential expressions [*see also p. 57*]:

Please can you ...	**Können Sie ... bitte?** kernnen zee ... bitteh
mince it?	**es durch den Fleischwolf drehen** es doorsh den flysh-volf dray-en
dice it?	**es in kleine Stücke schneiden** es in kly-neh shtoock-eh shnyden
trim the fat?	**das Fett abschneiden** das fett up-shnyden

Fish

ESSENTIAL INFORMATION

- The place to ask for: **EIN FISCHGESCHÄFT** (fish shop) or the **FISCHABTEILUNG** (fish section) in the food departments of larger stores.
- Look out also for **NORDSEE** – a fish shop chain selling fresh fish and smoked and marinated specialities as well as snack meals.
- Shellfish (**MEERESFRÜCHTE**) is quite rare in Germany.
- Large markets usually have fresh fish stalls.
- Weight guide: 8 oz/250 g minimum per person, for one meal of fish bought on the bone.
  i.e. ½ kilo/500 g for two people
  1 kilo   for four people
  1½ kilos   for six people

WHAT TO SAY

Purchase large fish and small shellfish by the weight:

1lb (½ kilo) of ...	**Ein Pfund ...**
	*i*ne pfoont ...
1 kilo of ...	**Ein Kilo ...**
	*i*ne k*i*lo ...
3lbs (1½ kilos) of ...	**Drei Pfund ...**
	dry pfoont ...
cod	**Kabeljau**
	k*a*hbel-yow
haddock	**Schellfisch**
	sh*e*ll-fish
turbot	**Steinbutt**
	sht*i*ne-boott
carp	**Karpfen**
	k*a*rp-fen
red sea-bass	**Rotbarsch**
	r*o*te-barsh
halibut	**Heilbutt**
	h*i*le-boott

3lbs (1½ kilos) of ...	**Drei Pfund ...**
	dry pfoont ...
pike	**Hecht**
	hesht
shrimps	**Garnelen**
	gar-nay-len
shrimps (N. Germany)	**Granat**
	grah-naht
prawns	**Krabben**
	krabben
mussels	**Muscheln**
	moosheln

Some large fish can be purchased by the slice:

One slice of ...	**Ein Stück ...**
	ine shtook ...
Two slices of ...	**Zwei Stück ...**
	tsvy shtook ...
Six slices of ...	**Sechs Stück ...**
	zex shtook ...
cod	**Kabeljau**
	kahbel-yow
haddock	**Schellfisch**
	shell-fish
halibut	**Heilbutt**
	hile-boott
Two slices of salmon	**Zwei Scheiben Lachs**
	tsvy shy-ben laks

For some shellfish and 'frying pan' fish, specify the number you want:

A crab, please	**Einen Krebs, bitte**
	inen kreps bitteh
A lobster	**Einen Hummer**
	inen hoommer
A spiny lobster	**Eine Languste**
	ineh langoost-eh
A plaice	**Eine Scholle**
	ineh sholl-eh
A trout	**Eine Forelle**
	ineh forell-eh

A sole	**Eine Seezunge**
	ineh zay-tsoong-eh
A mackerel	**Eine Makrele**
	ineh mak-raileh
A herring	**Einen Hering**
	inen hair-ing

Other essential expressions [*see also p. 57*]:

Please can you ...	**Können Sie, bitte ...**
	kernnen zee bitteh ...
take the heads off?	**Kopf und Schwanz entfernen?**
	kopf oont shvants ent-fairnen
clean them?	**den Fisch ausnehmen?**
	den fish ows-nay-men
fillet them?	**den Fisch in Scheiben schneiden?**
	den fish in shy-ben shny-den

Eating and drinking out

Ordering a drink

ESSENTIAL INFORMATION

- The places to ask for: **EIN CAFÉ** [see p. 19].
  EINE WIRTSCHAFT (a type of pub).
  EINE WEINSTUBE (a wine bar).
- By law, the price list of drinks (**GETRÄNKEKARTE**) must
  be displayed outside or in the window.
- There is always waiter service in cafés, pubs and wine bars. In
  a pub you can also drink at the bar if you wish (cheaper).
- A service charge of 10–15% is almost always included on the
  bill (**BEDIENUNG INBEGRIFFEN**), but it is customary to
  leave some additional small change.
- Cafés serve non-alcoholic and alcoholic drinks, and are
  normally open all day.

WHAT TO SAY

I'll have . . . please	**Ich hätte gern . . . bitte** ish hetteh gairn . . . bitteh
a black coffee	**einen schwarzen Kaffee** *i*nen shvar-tsen kaffeh
a coffee with cream	**einen Kaffee mit Sahne** *i*nen kaffeh mit zahneh
a tea	**einen Tee** *i*nen tay
with milk	**mit Milch** mit milsh
with lemon	**mit Zitrone** mit tsee-trone-eh
a glass of milk	**ein Glas Milch** ine glass milsh
two glasses of milk	**zwei Glas Milch** tsvy glass milsh
a hot chocolate	**eine heisse Schokolade** *i*neh hysseh shoko-lahdeh

a mineral water	**ein Mineralwasser**
	*i*ne miner*ah*l-vasser
a lemonade	**eine Limonade**
	*i*neh lim-o-n*ah*deh
a Coca Cola	**eine (Coca) Cola**
	*i*neh (coca) *co*la
an orangeade	**einen Orangensprudel**
	*i*nen o-r*u*ng-shen-shpr*oo*del
a fresh orange juice	**einen frischen Orangensaft**
	*i*nen fr*i*shen o-r*u*ng-shen-zaft
a grape juice	**einen Traubensaft**
	*i*nen tra-*oo*ben-zaft
an apple juice	**einen Apfelsaft**
	*i*nen *a*pfel-zaft
a beer	**ein Bier**
	*i*ne b*ee*r
a draught beer	**ein Bier vom Fass**
	*i*ne b*ee*r fom f*a*ss
a light ale	**ein helles Bier**
	*i*ne h*e*ll-es b*ee*r
a lager	**ein Pilsener**
	*i*ne p*i*l-zen-er
a bitter	**ein Altbier**
	*i*ne *a*lt-beer
a brown ale	**ein dunkles Bier**
	*i*ne d*oo*nk-les b*ee*r
a half	**ein Kleines**
	*i*ne kly-nes
A glass of ...	**Ein Glas ...**
	*i*ne glass
Two glasses of ...	**Zwei Glas ...**
	tsvy glass
red wine	**Rotwein**
	r*o*te-vine
white wine	**Weisswein**
	v*i*ce-vine
rosé wine	**Rosé**
	roz*ay*
dry	**herben**
	h*ai*r-ben
sweet	**süssen**
	s*oo*ossen

A bottle of ...	Eine Flasche ...
	*i*neh fl*a*sheh
sparkling wine	Schaumwein
	sh*a-oom*-vine
champagne (German)	Sekt
	z*e*kt
champagne (French)	Champagner
	sham-p*a*nyer
A whisky	Einen Whisky
	*i*nen v*i*sky
with ice	mit Eis
	mit *i*ce
with water	mit Wasser
	mit v*a*sser
with soda	mit Soda
	mit z*o*da
A gin	Einen Gin
	*i*nen gin
with tonic	mit Tonik
	mit t*o*nic
with bitter lemon	mit Bitter Lemon
	mit b*i*tter l*e*mon
A brandy/cognac	Einen Weinbrand/Cognac
	*i*nen v*i*ne-brant/con-y*a*c
A Martini	Einen Martini
	*i*nen mart*i*ni
A sherry	Einen Sherry
	*i*nen sh*e*rry

These are local drinks you may like to try:

ein Schnapps	a strong spirit distilled from
ine shn*a*ps	grain
eine Berliner Weisse	light Berlin ale with raspberry
*i*neh ber-l*ee*ner v*i*ce-eh	juice
ein Himbeergeist	raspberry brandy
ine h*i*m-bear-gyst	
ein Doppelbock/Märzen	strong Munich beers
ine d*o*ppel-bock/m*ai*r-tsen	
eine Altbierbowle	a bitter with bits of pineapple
*i*neh *a*lt-beer-boleh	
ein Kirschwasser	Black Forest brandy distilled
ine k*ee*rsh-vasser	from cherries

ein Grog ine grok	hot diluted rum with sugar
ein Glühwein ine gloo-vine	mulled wine
ein Malzbier ine malts-beer	dark sweet malt beer
ein Eierlikör ine eye-er-leeker	eggflip, eggnog

Other essential expressions:

Miss! [this does not sound abrupt in German]	**Fräulein!** froy-line
Waiter!	**Herr Ober!** hair o-ber
The bill, please	**Die Rechnung, bitte** dee resh-noong bitteh
How much does that come to?	**Wieviel macht das insgesamt?** vee-feel makt das ins-gazamt
Is service included?	**Ist Bedienung inbegriffen?** ist bedeenoong in-begriffen
Where is the toilet, please?	**Wo sind die Toiletten?** vo zint dee twa-letten

Ordering a snack

ESSENTIAL INFORMATION

- Look for any of these places:
  SCHNELLIMBISS ⎤
  IMBISSTUBE ⎦ (snack bar)
  BRATWURSTSTAND (sausage stall)
  HÄHNCHEN-GRILL (chicken takeaway; WIENERWALD
  is a popular chain)
  NORDSEE (a fish shop and takeaway chain found in larger
  towns)
- Apart from snacks, all these places sell soft drinks, canned or
  bottled beer, and also tea, coffee etc.
- Look for the names of snacks (listed below) on signs in the
  window or on the pavement.
- For cakes, see p. 62.
- For ice-cream, see p. 64.
- For picnic-type snacks, see p. 68.

WHAT TO SAY

I'll have . . . please	**Ich hätte gern . . . bitte** ish hetteh gairn . . . bitteh
a cheese sandwich/roll	**ein Käsebrot/Käsebrötchen** ine kaizeh-brote/kaizeh-brertshen

a ham sandwich/roll	**ein Schinkenbrot/**
	  Schinkenbrötchen
	ine shinken-brote/
	  shinken-brertshen

a roll with fish	**ein Fischbrötchen** ine fish-brertshen
an omelette	**ein Omelett** ine omelet
with mushrooms	**mit Pilzen** mit pil-tsen
with diced ham	**mit Schinken** mit shinken

These are some other snacks you may like to try:

eine Bratwurst
ineh br*ah*t-voorst
a fried spicy pork sausage

eine Bockwurst
ineh b*o*ck-voorst
a large Frankfurter

eine Currywurst
ineh c*u*rry-voorst
a grilled sausage topped with curry and ketchup

ein halbes Hähnchen
ine h*a*lbes h*ai*n-shen
half a (roast) chicken

ein Deutsches Beefsteak
ine d*oy*t-shes b*ee*fsteak
a Hamburger steak

ein Paar Spiegeleier
ine par shp*ee*g-el-eye-er
two fried eggs

eine Gulaschsuppe
ineh g*oo*lash-zooppeh
spicy beef soup

You may want to add to your order:

with bread, please	**mit Brot, bitte** mit br*o*te b*i*tteh
with chips	**mit Pommes Frites** mit pom fr*i*t
with potato salad	**mit Kartoffelsalat** mit kar-t*o*ffel-zal*ah*t
with (fried) onions	**mit Zwiebeln** mit tsv*ee*-beln
with mustard	**mit Senf** mit zenf
with ketchup	**mit Ketchup** mit k*e*tchup
with mayonnaise	**mit Mayonnaise** mit mayo-n*ai*zeh

[*For other essential expressions, see 'Ordering a drink', p. 80*]

In a restaurant

ESSENTIAL INFORMATION

- The place to ask for: **ein Restaurant** [see p. 19]
- You can eat at these places:
  RESTAURANT
  HOTEL-RESTAURANT
  GASTSTÄTTE/GASTHOF
  RASTHOF (motorway restaurant)
  GASTWIRTSCHAFT
  BAHNHOFSBÜFETT (at stations)
  GRILLSTUBE
  CAFÉ (limited choice here)
- By law, the menus must be displayed outside or in the window – and that is the *only* way to judge if a place is right for you.
- Self-service restaurants are not unknown, but most places have waiter service.
- A service charge of 10–15% is usually included in restaurant bills, but if satisfied with the service you should always leave some small change.
- Most restaurants offer small portions for children. Look for **KINDER-TELLER** (children's portions) on the menu.
- Hot meals are served from 12.00 to 2.00 p.m. at lunchtime and from 6.00 to 9.00–10.00 p.m. at night. After that many restaurants offer snacks for latecomers (soups, sausages, salads etc.) Ask for the 'small menu': **die kleine Karte** (dee kly-neh karteh).

WHAT TO SAY

May I book a table?	**Kann ich einen Tisch reservieren lassen?** kan ish *i*nen t*i*sh reser-v*ee*ren lassen
I've booked a table	**Ich habe einen Tisch reservieren lassen** ish h*a*hbeh *i*nen t*i*sh reser-v*ee*ren lassen

A table ...	**Einen Tisch ...**
	*i*nen t*i*sh ...
for one	**für eine Person**
	foor *i*neh per-zone
for three	**für drei Personen**
	foor dry per-zonen
The à la carte menu, please	**Die Speisekarte, bitte**
	dee shpyzeh-karteh b*i*tteh
The fixed-price menu	**Die Gedeck-Karte**
	dee gad*e*ck-karteh
The tourist menu	**Das Touristen-Menü**
	das tour*i*sten-men*oo*
Today's special menu	**Die Karte mit Tagesgedecken**
	dee karteh mit t*a*hg-es-gad*e*cken
What's this, please [*point to menu*]	**Was ist dies, bitte?**
	vas ist dees b*i*tteh
The wine list	**Die Weinkarte**
	dee v*i*ne-karteh
A carafe of wine, please	**Eine Karaffe Wein, bitte**
	*i*neh ka-r*a*ffeh v*i*ne b*i*tteh
A quarter (25cc)	**Einen Viertelliter**
	*i*nen f*ee*r-tel-litre
A half (50cc)	**Einen halben Liter**
	*i*nen h*a*lben l*i*tre
A glass	**Ein Glas**
	ine glass
A bottle	**Eine Flasche**
	*i*neh fl*a*sheh
A half-bottle	**Eine halbe Flasche**
	*i*neh h*a*lbeh fl*a*sheh
A litre	**Einen Liter**
	*i*nen l*i*tre
Red/white/rosé/house wine	**Rotwein/Weisswein/Rosé/ Hauswein**
	rote-vine/v*i*ce-vine/roz*a*y house-vine
Some more bread, please	**Noch etwas Brot, bitte**
	nok *e*tvas brote b*i*tteh
Some more wine	**Noch etwas Wein**
	nok *e*tvas v*i*ne
Some oil	**Etwas Öl**
	*e*tvas erl

Some vinegar	**Etwas Essig** *etvas* essick
Some salt	**Etwas Salz** *etvas* zalts
Some pepper	**Etwas Pfeffer** *etvas* pf*effer*
Some water	**Etwas Wasser** *etvas* v*asser*
How much does that come to?	**Wieviel macht das insgesamt?** vee-feel makt das ins-gaz*amt*
Is service included?	**Ist Bedienung inbegriffen?** ist be-dee-n-oong *in*-begriffen
Where is the toilet, please?	**Wo sind dieToiletten?** vo zint dee twa-l*etten*
Miss! [*This does not sound abrupt in German*]	**Fräulein!** froy-line
Waiter!	**Herr Ober!** hair *o*-ber
The bill, please	**Die Rechnung, bitte** dee resh-noong b*itteh*

Key words for courses, as seen on some menus

[*Only ask this question if you want the waiter to remind you of the choice.*]

What have you got in the way of . . .	**Was für . . . haben Sie?** vas foor . . . h*ahben* zee
STARTERS?	**VORSPEISEN** for-shpyzen
SOUP?	**SUPPEN** z*oo*ppen
EGG DISHES?	**EIERSPEISEN** *eye*-er-shpyzen
FISH?	**FISCHGERICHTE** fish-garisht-eh
MEAT?	**FLEISCHGERICHTE** flysh-garisht-eh
GAME?	**WILDGERCHTE** vilt-garisht-eh
FOWL?	**GEFLÜGELGERICHTE** ga-fl*oo*gel-garisht-eh
VEGETABLES?	**GEMÜSE** ga-m*oo*zeh

CHEESE?	**KÄSE**
	k*a*y-zeh
FRUIT?	**OBST**
	opst
ICE-CREAM?	**EIS**
	ice
DESSERT?	**NACHSPEISEN**
	n*a*hk-shpyzen

UNDERSTANDING THE MENU

You will find the names of the principal ingredients of most dishes on these pages:

Starters, see p. 68

Fruit, see p. 71

Meat, see p. 75

Dessert, see p. 62

Fish, see p. 77

Cheese, see p. 68

Vegetables, see p. 71

Ice-cream, see p. 64

Used together with the following lists of cooking and menu terms, they should help you to decode the menu.
(These cooking and menu terms are for understanding only – not for speaking aloud.)

Cooking and menu terms

angemacht	in a special dressing
Auflauf	soufflé
blau	steamed and served with butter
blutig	rare
Bouillon	broth, clear soup
Brat–	fried
–braten	roast, joint
–brühe	broth
–brust	breast
Butter–	buttered
durchgebraten	well done
gebacken	baked
gedämpft	steamed
gedünstet (Austria)	steamed, stewed
gefüllt	stuffed
gegrillt	grilled
gekocht	boiled
in Gelee	jellied

gemischt	mixed
gepökelt	salted, pickled
geräuchert	smoked
gerieben	grated
geschmort	braised, stewed
gespickt	larded, smoked
halbdurch	medium
Hausfrauenart	with apple, sour cream and onions
hausgemacht	homemade
Holländisch	with mayonnaise
Holstein	topped with fried egg, garnished with anchovies and vegetables
Jägerart	served in red wine sauce with mushrooms
–Kaltschale	chilled fruit soup
–Kompott	stewed fruit
Kraftbrühe	broth, beef consommé
Kräuter–	with herbs
mariniert	marinated
Meerrettich–	with horse radish
Müllerin	baked in butter, dressed with breadcrumbs and egg
paniert	dressed with egg and breadcrumbs
Pell–	boiled in the jacket
Petersilien–	parsleyed
–püree	mashed
Rahm–	with cream
roh	raw
Röst–	fried
Sahne–	creamed
sauer	sour
Schlemmer–	for the gourmet
Schnitzel	escalope (of veal)
Senf–	with mustard
Sosse	sauce
Sülz–	in aspic
süss	sweet
überbacken	au gratin
Zwiebel–	with onions

Further words to help you understand the menu

Aalsuppe	eel soup, a speciality of Hamburg
Aufschnitt	sliced cold meat and sausages
Austern	oysters
Bauernomelett	bacon and onion omelette
Bierwurst	beer sausage
Birne Helene	vanilla ice-cream with pear and hot chocolate sauce
Bismarckhering	soused herring with onions
Blutwurst	black pudding
Bockwurst	large Frankfurter sausage
Bratkartoffeln	fried potatoes
Bratwurst	fried sausage (with herbs)
Deutsches Beefsteak	Hamburger steak
Eisbein	pig's knuckle
Ente	duck
Erbsensuppe	thick pea soup
Fasan	pheasant
Fleischkäse	type of meatloaf, sliced and fried
Forelle	trout
Frühlingssuppe	fresh vegetable soup
Gänseleberpastete	goose liver pâté
Gefrorenes	ice-cream specialities
Grünkohl	kale
Hackbraten	Hamburger steak
Kaiserschmarren	shredded pancake with raisins and almonds
Kartoffelpuffer	small potato and onion pancakes
Kasseler Rippenspeer	cured pork chops with mustard sauce
Klösse **Knödel**	dumplings
Königsberger Klopse	meat balls in a white caper sauce
Kohlrouladen	cabbage stuffed with minced meat
Labskaus	pork and potato stew served with fried eggs and gherkins
Lachs	salmon
Leberknödelsuppe	soup with liver dumplings
Leberwurst	liver pâté
Linsensuppe	lentil soup

Matjeshering	young salted herring
Ochsenschwanzsuppe	oxtail soup
Ölsardinen	tinned sardines
Paprikaschoten	green peppers
Pfannkuchen	pancake
Pfirsich Melba	peach with vanilla ice-cream, whipped cream, raspberry syrup
Räucheraal	smoked eel
Rauchwurst	smoked sausage
Rehrücken	saddle of deer
Rollmops	pickled herring fillet, rolled around onion slices
Rosenkohl	Brussels sprouts
Rösti	hashed brown potatoes
Röstkartoffeln	roast potatoes
Rote Beete	beetroot
Rotkraut	red cabbage
Rouladen	thin slices of meat, rolled up and braised in rich brown sauce
Russische Eier	hard-boiled eggs, with caper and mayonnaise dressing
Sardellen	anchovies
Sauerkraut	pickled white cabbage
Sauerbraten	beef marinated in vinegar, sugar and spices, and then braised
Schildkrötensuppe	turtle soup
Schinkenwurst	ham sausage
Schlachtplatte	assorted cold meat and sausages
Schweinshaxe	pig's knuckle
Serbische Bohnensuppe	spicy Serbian bean soup
Spargel	asparagus
Spätzle	South German variety of pasta
Speck	bacon
Strammer Max	raw ham and fried eggs, served on rye-bread
Truthahn	turkey
Weinbergschnecken	snails with garlic, herbs and butter
Wienerschnitzel	veal escalope in breadcrumbs

Health

ESSENTIAL INFORMATION

- For details of reciprocal health agreements between the UK and Germany, Austria and Switzerland, ask for leaflet SA 30 at your local Department of Health and Social Security a month before leaving or ask your travel agent.
- In addition it is preferable to purchase a medical insurance policy through the travel agent, a broker or a motoring organization.
- Take your own 'first line' first aid kit with you.
- For minor disorders, and treatment at a chemist's, see p. 41.
- For finding your way to a doctor, dentist, chemist or Health and Social Security Office (for reimbursement), see p. 19.
- Once in Germany, Austria or Switzerland decide on a definite plan of action in case of serious illness: communicate your problem to a near neighbour, the receptionist or someone you see regularly. You are then dependent on that person helping you obtain treatment.
- In an emergency dial 110 for an ambulance service.
- If you need a doctor look for:
  ÄRTZE (in the telephone directory) or these signs:
  PRAXIS (surgery)
  ERSTE HILFE (first aid)
  KRANKENHAUS ⎤
  HOSPITAL ⎦ (hospital)
  UNFALLSTATION (casualty department of a hospital)

What's the matter?

I have a pain in my ...	Ich habe Schmerzen ...
	ish hahbeh shmairts-en ...
abdomen	im Unterleib
	im oonter-lipe
ankle	im Fussgelenk
	im fooss-galenk
arm	im Arm
	im arm
back	im Rücken
	im roocken
bladder	an der Blase
	un der blah-zeh

I have a pain in my ...	Ich habe Schmerzen ...
	ish hahbeh shmairts-en ...
bowels	im Darm
	im darm
breast	in der Brust
	in der broost
chest	im Brustkorb
	im broost-korp
ear	im Ohr
	im or
eye	im Auge
	im owg-eh
foot	am Fuss
	um fooss
head	im Kopf
	im kopf
heel	an der Ferse
	un der fair-zeh
jaw	im Kiefer
	im keefer
kidneys	an den Nieren
	un den neeren
leg	im Bein
	im bine
lung	in der Lunge
	in der loong-eh
neck	im Genick
	im ganick
penis	im Penis
	im painis
shoulder	in der Schulter
	in der shoolter
stomach	im Magen
	im mah-ghen
testicles	in den Hoden
	in den hoden
throat	im Hals
	im hals
vagina	in der Vagina
	in der vahg-ee-nah
wrist	im Handgelenk
	im hant-galenk
I have a pain here [point]	Ich habe hier Schmerzen
	ish hahbeh here shmairts-en

I have a toothache	**Ich habe Zahnschmerzen**
	ish h*a*hbeh ts*a*hn-shmairts-en
I have broken my dentures	**Mein Gebiss ist zerbrochen**
	mine gab*i*s ist tsair-br*o*cken
I have broken my glasses	**Meine Brille ist zerbrochen**
	m*i*neh br*i*lleh ist tsair-br*o*cken
I have lost ...	**Ich habe ... verloren**
	ish h*a*hbeh ... fer-l*o*ren
my contact lenses	**meine Kontaktlinsen**
	m*i*neh kont*a*kt-lin-zen
a filling	**eine Füllung**
	*i*neh f*oo*lloong
My child is ill	**Mein Kind ist krank**
	mine k*i*nt ist krank
He/she has a pain in	**Er/sie hat Schmerzen ...**
his/her ...	air/zee hat shm*ai*rts-en
ankle [see list above]	**im Fussgelenk**
	im f*oo*ss-galenk

How bad is it?

I'm ill	**Ich bin krank**
	ish bin kr*a*nk
It's urgent	**Es ist dringend**
	es ist dr*i*ng-ent
It's serious	**Es ist etwas Ernstes**
	es ist *e*tvas *ai*rnstes
It's not serious	**Es ist nichts Ernstes**
	es ist n*i*shts *ai*rnstes
It hurts	**Es tut weh**
	es toot v*a*y
It hurts a lot	**Es tut sehr weh**
	es toot z*ai*r vay
It doesn't hurt much	**Es tut nicht sehr weh**
	es toot n*i*sht zair vay
The pain occurs ...	**Der Schmerz tritt ... auf**
	der shm*ai*rts trit ... owf
every quarter of an hour	**alle Viertelstunde**
	*a*lleh f*ee*rtel-shtoondeh
every half-hour	**alle halbe Stunde**
	*a*lleh h*a*lbeh shtoondeh
every hour	**jede Stunde**
	y*a*ideh sht*oo*ndeh
every day	**jeden Tag**
	y*a*iden t*a*hk

The pain occurs . . .	**Der Schmerz tritt . . . auf**
	der shmairts trit . . . owf
most of the time	**fast ununterbrochen**
	fast oon-oonter-brocken
I've had it for . . .	**Ich habe es seit . . .**
	ish hahbeh es zite . . .
one hour/one day	**einer Stunde/einem Tag**
	iner shtoondeh/inem tahk
two hours/two days	**zwei Stunden/zwei Tagen**
	tsvy shtoonden/tsvy tahg-en
It's a . . .	**Es ist ein . . .**
	es ist ine . . .
sharp pain	**stechender Schmerz**
	shteshen-der shmairts
dull ache	**dumpfer Schmerz**
	doompfer shmairts
nagging pain	**bohrender Schmerz**
	boren-der shmairts
I feel dizzy/sick	**Mir ist schwindlig/übel**
	meer ist shvindlik/oobel
I feel weak/feverish	**Ich fühle mich schwach/fieberig**
	ish fooleh mish shvak/feeb-rik

Already under treatment for something else?

I take . . . regularly [*show*]	**Ich nehme regelmässig . . .**
	ish nay-meh raig-el-masik . . .
this medicine	**dieses Medikament**
	deezes medikament
these tablets	**diese Tabletten**
	deezeh tabletten
I have . . .	**Ich habe . . .**
	ish hahbeh . . .
a heart condition	**ein Herzleiden**
	ine hairts-ly-den
haemorrhoids	**Hämorrhoiden**
	hemorro-ee-den
rheumatism	**Rheuma**
	roymah
I'm . . .	**Ich bin . . .**
	ish bin . . .
diabetic	**Diabetiker**
	dee-ah-beticker

asthmatic	**Asthmatiker** ast-m*a*h-ticker
pregnant	**schwanger** shv*a*nger
allergic to (penicillin)	**allergisch gegen (Penicillin)** all*ai*r-gish g*a*y-ghen (peni-tsee-l*ee*n)

Other essential expressions

Please can you help?	**Können Sie bitte helfen?** k*er*nnen zee b*i*tteh h*e*lfen
A doctor, please	**Einen Arzt, bitte** *i*nen *a*rtst b*i*tteh
A dentist	**Einen Zahnarzt** *i*nen ts*a*hn-artst
I don't speak German	**Ich spreche nicht deutsch** ish shpr*e*sheh nisht d*o*ytsh
What time does . . . arrive?	**Um wieviel Uhr kommt . . . ?** oom v*ee*feel *oo*r kommt
the doctor	**der Arzt** der *a*rtst
the dentist	**der Zahnarzt** der ts*a*hn-artst

From the doctor: key sentences to understand

Take this . . .	**Nehmen Sie dies . . .** n*ay*-men zee d*ee*s . . .
every day/hour	**täglich/stündlich** t*ai*k-lish/sht*oo*nt-lish
twice/three times a day	**zweimal/dreimal pro Tag** tsv*y*-mal/dr*y*-mal pro t*a*hk
Stay in bed	**Bleiben Sie im Bett** bl*y*-ben zee im bet
Don't travel . . .	**Reisen Sie nicht . . .** r*y*zen zee n*i*sht . . .
for . . . days/weeks	**in den nächsten . . . Tagen/ Wochen** in den n*e*ksten . . . t*a*hg-en/v*o*k-en
You must go to hospital	**Sie müssen ins Krankenhaus** zee m*oo*ssen ins kr*a*nken-house

Problems: complaints, loss, theft

ESSENTIAL INFORMATION

- Problems with:
  camping facilities, see p. 35   health, p. 93
  household appliances, see p. 39   the car, see p. 109
- If the worst comes to the worst, find the police station. To ask the way, see p. 19.
- Look for:
  POLIZEI (police)
  POLIZEIWACHE (police station)
- Ask for:
  FUNDBÜRO (lost property)
- If you lose your passport go to the nearest British Consulate.
- In an emergency dial 110 (for police) or 112 (if there's a fire).

COMPLAINTS

I bought this ...	**Ich habe dies ... gekauft** ish hahbeh dees ... ga-kowft
today	**heute** hoy-teh
yesterday	**gestern** ghestern
on Monday [see p. 133]	**Montag** mone-tahk
It's no good	**Es ist nicht in Ordnung** es ist nisht in ort-noong
Look	**Sehen Sie** zay-en zee
Here [point]	**Hier** here
Can you ...	**Können Sie ...** kernnen zee
change it?	**es umtauschen?** es oom-towshen
mend it?	**es in Ordnung bringen?** es in ort-noong bring-en
Here's the receipt	**Hier ist der Kassenzettel** here ist der kassen-tsettel

Can I have a refund?	**Kann ich das Geld zurückbekommen?** kan ish das ghelt tsoo-*rook*-bekommen
Can I see the manager?	**Kann ich den Geschäftsführer sprechen?** kan ish den gashefts-foorer shpreshen

LOSS

[See also 'Theft' below: the lists are interchangeable]

I have lost ...	**Ich habe ... verloren** ish hahbeh ... fer-loren
my bag	**meine Handtasche** mineh han-tasheh
my bracelet	**mein Armband** mine arm-bant
my camera	**meine Kamera** mineh kamerah
my car keys	**meine Autoschlüssel** mineh owto-shloossel
my car logbook	**meinen Kraftfahrzeugschein** minen kraft-far-tsoyk-shine
my driving licence	**meinen Führerschein** minen foorer-shine
my insurance certificate	**meine Versicherungskarte** mineh fer-zisheroongs-karteh
my jewellery	**meinen Schmuck** minen shmoock
my keys	**meine Schlüssel** mineh shloossel
everything!	**alle meine Sachen!** alleh mineh zakhen

THEFT

[See also 'Loss' above: the lists are interchangeable]

Someone has stolen ...	**Man hat ... gestohlen** man hat ... ga-shtolen
my car	**mein Auto** mine owto
my car radio	**mein Autoradio** mine owto-rahdio

Someone has stolen . . .	Man hat . . . gestohlen
	man hat . . . ga-shtolen
my money	mein Geld
	mine ghelt
my necklace	meine Halskette
	mineh hals-ketteh
my passport	meinen Pass
	minen pass
my radio	mein Radio
	mine rahdio
my tickets	meine Fahrkarten
	mineh far-karten
my travellers' cheques	meine Reiseschecks
	mineh ryzeh-shecks
my wallet	meine Brieftasche
	mineh breef-tasheh
my watch	meine Uhr
	mineh oor
my luggage	mein Gepäck
	mine gapeck

LIKELY REACTIONS: key words to understand

Wait	Warten Sie, bitte
	varten zee bitteh
When?	Wann?
	vann
Where?	Wo?
	vo
Your name?	Ihr Name?
	eer nahmeh
Address?	Adresse/Anschrift?
	ah-dresseh/un-shrift
I can't help you	Ich kann Ihnen nicht helfen
	ish kan eenen nisht helf-en
Nothing to do with me	Ich bin dafür nicht zuständig
	ish bin dafoor nisht tsoo-shtendik

The post office

ESSENTIAL INFORMATION

- To find a post office, see p. 19.
- Key words to look for:
  POST
  POSTAMT
  BUNDESPOST
- Look for this sign.

- For stamps look for the words **BRIEFMARKEN** or **POSTWERTZEICHEN** on a post office counter.
- Some stationers' and kiosks which sell postcards, also sell stamps.
- Letter boxes in Germany, Switzerland and Austria are yellow, but you may still find some blue ones in Austria. A red point on some letter boxes indicates that they are emptied frequently, late at night (**SPÄTLEERUNG**) and also on Sundays.
- Plain stamped postcards and stamps can also be obtained from yellow vending machines situated outside post offices or at the back of phone boxes. Ask for **BRIEFMARKEN AUTOMAT** or look for the word **WERTZEICHENGEBER**.
- For poste restante you should show your passport at the counter marked **POSTLAGERNDE SENDUNGEN** in the main post office: a small fee is usually payable.

WHAT TO SAY

To England, please	**Nach England, bitte**
	nahk eng-lant bitteh

[Hand letters, cards or parcels over the counter]

To Australia	**Nach Australien**
	nahk owstrah-lee-en
To the United States	**In die Vereinigten Staaten**
	in dee ferine-nik-ten shtahten

[For other countries, see p. 137]

How much is ...	**Wieviel kostet ...**
	vee-feel k*o*stet ...
this parcel (to Canada)?	**dieses Paket (nach Kanada)?**
	d*ee*zes pah-k*a*te (nahk k*a*nadah)
a letter (to Australia)?	**ein Brief (nach Australien)?**
	ine br*ee*f (nahk owstr*a*h-lee-en)
a postcard (to England)?	**eine Postkarte (nach England)?**
	*i*neh p*o*st-karteh (nahk *e*ng-lant)
Airmail	**Luftpost**
	l*oo*ft-post
Surface mail	**Normaler Tarif**
	norm*a*h-ler tah-r*ee*f
One stamp, please	**Eine Briefmarke, bitte**
	*i*neh br*ee*f-markeh b*i*tteh
Two stamps	**Zwei Briefmarken**
	tsv*y* br*ee*f-marken
One (50) Pfennig stamp	**Eine Briefmarke zu (fünfzig) Pfennig**
	*i*neh br*ee*f-markeh tsoo (f*oo*nf-tsik) pfennik
I'd like to send a telegram	**Ich möchte ein Telegramm aufgeben**
	ish m*e*rshteh ine tele-gr*a*m *o*wf-gaiben

Telephoning

ESSENTIAL INFORMATION

- Public phone boxes (**ÖFFENTLICHER FERNSPRECHER**) are painted yellow and take coins. Foreign calls can only be made from boxes marked with a green disc and the words **INTERNATIONAL** or **AUSLAND**. This is how to use a public telephone:
  - take off the receiver
  - insert the money
  - dial the number (unused coins will be refunded)

- For a call to the UK dial 0044; the code to the USA is 001.

- If you need a number abroad ring inquiries (**AUSKUNFT**) 00118. They normally speak English.

- For calls to countries which cannot be dialled direct go to a post office and write the country, town and number you want on a piece of paper. Add **MIT VORANMELDUNG** if you want a person-to-person call or **R-GESPRÄCH** if you want to reverse the charges.

- Before travelling abroad, ask at your local post office for details of phoning England from abroad.

- If you have difficulty in making a phone call, go to the post office and get them to put the call through (see above).

WHAT TO SAY

Where can I make a telephone call?	**Wo kann ich telefonieren?** vo kan ish tele-foneeren
Local/abroad	**Ein Ortsgespräch/ein Auslandsgespräch** ine orts-gashpraish/ine ows-lants-gashpraish

I'd like this number ...	**Ich möchte diese Nummer ...**
[*show number*]	ish m*e*rshteh d*ee*zeh n*oo*mmer ...
in England	**in England**
	in *e*ng-lant
in Canada	**in Kanada**
	in k*a*nadah
in the USA	**in den Vereinigten Staaten**
	in den fer*i*ne-nik-ten sht*a*hten

[*For other countries, see p. 137*]

Can you dial it for me, please?	**Können Sie für mich wählen?**
	k*e*rnnen zee foor mish v*a*y-len
How much is it?	**Wieviel kostet es?**
	v*ee*-feel k*o*stet es
Hello!	**Hallo!**
	h*u*llo
May I speak to ...?	**Kann ich ... sprechen?**
	kan ish ... shpr*e*shen
Extension ...	**Apparat ...**
	appar*a*ht ...
I'm sorry, I don't speak German	**Es tut mir leid, ich spreche nicht Deutsch**
	es toot meer l*i*te ish shpr*e*sheh nisht d*o*ytsh
Do you speak English?	**Sprechen Sie Englisch?**
	shpr*e*shen zee *e*ng-lish
Thank you, I'll phone back	**Danke, ich rufe wieder an**
	d*a*nkeh ish r*oo*feh v*ee*der un
Good-bye	**Auf Wiederhören**
	owf v*ee*der-hern

LIKELY REACTIONS

That's (4) marks (50)	**Das macht (vier) Mark (fünfzig)**
	das makt (f*ee*r) mark (f*oo*nf-tsik)
Cabin number (3)	**Kabine Nummer (drei)**
	kab*ee*neh n*oo*mmer (dr*y*)

[*For numbers, see p. 129*]

Don't hang up	**Bleiben Sie am Apparat** bl*y*ben zee am appa-*rah*t
I'm trying to connect you	**Ich verbinde Sie** ish fer-b*i*n-deh zee
You're through	**Hier ist Ihre Verbindung** here ist *ee*reh fer-b*i*n-doong
There's a delay	**Sie müssen warten** zee m*oo*ssen v*a*rten
I'll try again	**Ich versuche es noch einmal** ish fer-*zoo*keh es nok *i*ne-mahl

Changing cheques and money

ESSENTIAL INFORMATION

- Finding your way to a bank or change bureau, see p. 19.
- Look for these words on buildings:
  BANK (bank)
  SPARKASSE (bank, savings-bank)
  WECHSELSTUBE
  GELDWECHSEL } (change bureau)
- Banks are normally open from 8.00 a.m. to 12.30 p.m. and from 2.30 to 4.00 p.m. on weekdays. On Thursdays they stay open until 5.30 p.m. They are closed on Saturdays and Sundays.
- Change bureaux at frontier posts, airports and larger railway stations are usually open outside regular banking hours.
- Changing money or travellers' cheques is usually a two-stage process. The formalities are completed at a desk called **DEVISEN**; you will then be sent to the cashier (**KASSE**) to get your money.
- To cash your own normal cheques, exactly as at home, use your banker's card where you see the Eurocheque sign. Write in English, in pounds.
- Exchange rate information might show the pound as: **£**, **£ Sterling**, or even **GB**.
- Have your passport handy.

WHAT TO SAY

I'd like to cash . . .	**Ich möchte . . . einlösen**
	ish m*e*rshteh . . . *i*ne-lerzen
this travellers' cheque	**diesen Reisescheck**
	d*ee*zen ryzeh-sheck
these travellers' cheques	**diese Reiseschecks**
	d*ee*zeh ryzeh-shecks
this cheque	**diesen Scheck**
	d*ee*zen sheck
I'd like to change this into German marks	**Ich möchte dies in deutsche Mark wechseln**
	ish m*e*rshteh dees in d*o*ytsheh mark v*e*xeln

Here's ...	Hier ist ...
	here ist ...
my banker's card	meine Scheckkarte
	mineh sheck-karteh
my passport	mein Pass
	mine pass

For excursions into neighbouring countries

I'd like to change this ...	Ich möchte dies ... wechseln
[*show bank notes*]	*ish mershteh dees ... vexeln*
into Austrian schillings	in österreichische Schillinge
	in erster-ry-kisheh shilling-eh
into Belgian francs	in belgische Franken
	in bel-ghish-eh franken
into Danish kroner	in dänische Kronen
	in da-nisheh kro-nen
into Dutch guilders	in holländische Gulden
	in hollendisheh gool-den
into French francs	in französische Franken
	in fran-tser-zisheh franken
into Swiss francs	in Schweizer Franken
	in shvytser franken
What's the rate of exchange?	Wie ist der Wechselkurs?
	vee ist der vexel-koors

LIKELY REACTIONS

Your passport, please	Ihren Pass, bitte
	eeren pass bitteh
Sign here	Unterschreiben Sie hier
	oonter-shryben zee here
Your banker's card, please	Ihre Scheckkarte, bitte
	eereh sheck-karteh bitteh
Go to the cash desk	Gehen Sie zur Kasse
	gay-en zee tsoor kasseh

Car travel

ESSENTIAL INFORMATION

- Finding a filling station or garage, see p. 19.
- Is it a self-service station? Look out for:
  SELBSTBEDIENUNG or **SB**.
- Grades of petrol:
  BENZIN
  NORMAL] (standard)
  SUPER (premium)
  DIESEL
  MOTORRADÖL
  MEHRBEREICHSÖL] (two-stroke)
- 1 gallon is about 4½ litres (accurate enough up to 6 gallons).
- The minimum sale is often 5 litres (often less at self-service pumps).
- Filling stations are usually able to deal with minor mechanical problems. For major repairs you have to find a garage (**REPARATURWERKSTATT**).
- Unfamiliar road signs and warnings, see p. 123.

WHAT TO SAY
[For numbers, see p. 129]

(9) litres of ...	**(Neun) Liter ...**
	(noyn) li*tre* ...
(20) marks of ...	**Für (zwanzig) Mark ...**
	foor (tsv*a*n-tsik) mark ...
standard	**Normal**
	nor-m*ah*l
premium	**Super**
	z*oo*per
diesel	**Diesel**
	d*ee*zel
Fill it up, please	**Volltanken, bitte**
	f*o*lltanken b*i*tteh
Will you check ...	**Bitte prüfen Sie ...**
	b*i*tteh pr*oo*fen zee ...
the oil	**das Öl**
	das *er*l

the battery	**die Batterie**
	dee batter*ee*
the radiator	**das Kühlwasser**
	das k*oo*l-vasser
the tyres	**die Reifen**
	dee r*y*fen
I've run out of petrol	**Ich habe kein Benzin mehr**
	ish h*a*hbeh kine ben-ts*een* mair
Can I borrow a can, please?	**Können Sie mir einen Kanister leihen?**
	k*e*rnnen zee meer *i*nen kan*i*ster l*y*-en
My car has broken down	**Ich habe eine Panne**
	ish h*a*hbeh *i*neh p*a*nneh
My car won't start	**Mein Wagen springt nicht an**
	mine v*a*hg-en shpr*i*nkt nisht *u*n
I've had an accident	**Ich habe einen Unfall gehabt**
	ish h*a*hbeh *i*nen *oo*n-fal gah*a*pt
I've lost my car keys	**Ich habe meine Autoschlüssel verloren**
	ish h*a*hbeh mineh *o*wto-shlo*o*ssel fer-l*o*ren
My car is . . .	**Mein Wagen steht . . .**
	mine v*a*hg-en shtait . . .
one kilometre away	**einen Kilometer von hier**
	*i*nen kilo-m*a*ter fon h*e*re
three kilometres away	**drei Kilometer von hier**
	dr*y* kilo-m*a*ter fon h*e*re
Can you help me, please?	**Können Sie mir bitte helfen?**
	k*e*rnnen zee meer b*i*tteh h*e*lf-en
Do you do repairs?	**Machen Sie Reparaturen?**
	m*a*k-en zee repara-t*oo*ren
I have a puncture	**Ich habe eine Reifenpanne**
	ish h*a*hbeh *i*neh r*y*fen-panneh
I have a broken windscreen	**Die Windschutzscheibe ist zerbrochen**
	dee v*i*nt-shoots-shybeh ist tsair-br*o*cken
I don't know what's wrong	**Ich weiss nicht, woran es liegt**
	ish v*i*ce nisht vor*a*n es leekt
I think the problem is here . . . [*point*]	**Ich glaube, es liegt hieran . . .**
	ish gl*a*-oobeh es leekt h*e*re-un . . .

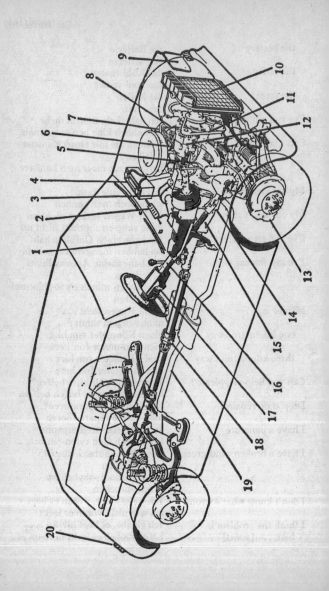

1 windscreen wipers	Scheibenwischer
	shyben-visher
2 fuses	Sicherungen
	zisher-oon-gen
3 heater	Heizung
	hy-tsoong
4 battery	Batterie
	batteree
5 engine	Motor
	mo-tore
6 fuel pump	Benzinpumpe
	ben-tseen-poompeh
7 starter motor	Anlasser
	un-lasser
8 carburettor	Vergaser
	fer-gahzer
9 lights	Scheinwerfer
	shine-vairfer
10 radiator	Kühler
	kooler
11 fan belt	Keilriemen
	kile-reemen
12 generator	Lichtmaschine
	lisht-masheeneh
13 brakes	Bremsen
	brem-zen
14 clutch	Kupplung
	koop-loong
15 gear box	Getriebe(block)
	ga-treebe(block)
16 steering	Lenkung
	lenk-oong
17 ignition	Zündung
	tsoon-doong
18 transmission	(Schalt-Getriebe
	(shalt)gatreebeh
19 exhaust	Auspuff
	ows-poof
20 indicators	Blinker
	blinker

Can you . . .   Können Sie . . .
                                 kernnen zee . . .

  repair the fault?   es reparieren?
                                 es repareeren

  come and look?   es sich ansehen?
                                 es zish un-zay-en

  estimate the cost?   einen Kostenvoranschlag
                                   machen?
                                 inen kosten-for-unshlahk mak-en

  write it down?   es aufschreiben?
                                 es owf-shryben

How long will the repair   Wie lange wird die Reparatur
take?   dauern?
                                 vee langeh veert dee repara-toor
                                   dowern

When will the car be ready?   Wann wird der Wagen fertig
                                   sein?
                                 vann veert der vahg-en fair-tik
                                   zine

Can I see the bill?   Kann ich die Rechnung sehen?
                                 kan ish dee resh-noong zay-en

This is my insurance   Hier ist meine Versicherungskarte
document   here ist mineh
                                   fer-zisheroongs-karteh

HIRING A CAR

Can I hire a car?   Kann ich einen Wagen mieten?
                                 kan ish inen vahg-en meeten

I need a car . . .   Ich brauche einen Wagen . . .
                                 ish browkeh inen vahg-en . . .

  for two people   für zwei Personen
                                 foor tsvy per-zonen

  for five people   für fünf Personen
                                 foor foonf per-zonen

  for one day   für einen Tag
                                 foor inen tahk

  for five days   für fünf Tage
                                 foor foonf tahg-eh

  for a week   für eine Woche
                                 foor ineh vok-eh

Can you write down ...	**Können Sie mir ...** **aufschreiben?** *kernnen zee meer ... owf-shryben*
the deposit to pay?	**die Kautionssumme** *dee kow-tsee-ons-zoommeh*
the charge per kilometre?	**die Gebühr pro Kilometer** *dee gaboor pro kilo-mater*
the daily charge?	**die Gebühr pro Tag** *dee gaboor pro tahk*
the cost of insurance?	**die Versicherungskosten** *dee fer-zisheroongs-kosten*
Can I leave it in (Hamburg)?	**Kann ich ihn in (Hamburg)** **abliefern?** *kan ish een in (hum-boorg) up-leefern*
What documents do I need?	**Was für Unterlagen brauche ich?** *vas foor oonter-lahg-en browkeh ish*

LIKELY REACTIONS

I don't do repairs	**Wir machen keine Reparaturen** *veer mak-en kineh repara-tooren*
Where's your car?	**Wo steht Ihr Wagen?** *vo shtait eer vahg-en*
What make is it?	**Was für ein Wagen ist es?** *vas foor ine vahg-en ist es*
Come back tomorrow/on Monday	**Kommen Sie morgen/Montag** **wieder** *kommen zee morgen/mone-tahk veeder*

[For days of the week, see p. 133]

We don't hire cars	**Wir vermieten keine Wagen** *veer fer-meeten kineh vahg-en*
Your driving licence, please	**Ihren Führerschein, bitte** *eeren foorer-shine bitteh*
The mileage is unlimited	**Die Kilometerzahl ist unbegrenzt** *dee kilo-mater-tsahl ist oon-begrentst*

Public transport

ESSENTIAL INFORMATION

- Finding the way to the bus station, a bus stop, a tram stop, the railway station and a taxi rank, see p. 19.
- Remember that queuing for buses is unheard of!
- To get a taxi you usually have to telephone the local **TAXIZENTRALE** (taxi centre) or go to a taxi rank. Hailing a taxi is less common and doesn't always work.
- Types of trains:
  TEE (Trans-Europe-Express; luxury high-speed train with first class only)
  INTERCITY
  EXPRESS
  SCHNELLZUG ⎤ (long distance trains, often between
  D-ZUG ⎥ countries, stopping only at principal stations)
  EILZUG (medium-distance, internal train, stopping only at bigger towns)
  PERSONENZUG (slow local train, stopping at all stations)
  NAHVERKEHRSZUG (short distance train, often to suburbs)
- Key words on signs: [see also p. 123]
  FAHRKARTEN (tickets, ticket office)
  EINGANG (entrance)
  AUSGANG (exit)
  VERBOTEN (forbidden)
  GLEIS (platform, literally: track)
  BAHNSTEIG (platform)
  BAHNHOFSMISSION (Travellers' Aid Office)
  AUSKUNFT (information, information office)
  DB (initials for German railways)
  GEPÄCKAUFBEWAHRUNG (left-luggage)
  BUSHALTESTELLE (bus-stop)
  ABFAHRT (timetable, departures)
  ANKUNFT (timetable, arrivals)
  GEPÄCKABFERTIGUNG ⎤ (luggage office/forwarding office
  GEPÄCKANNAHME ⎦
- Buying a ticket:
  Buy your train ticket at the ticket office inside the station. When travelling by bus or tram you usually pay as you enter.

When travelling by underground (**U-BAHN**) you buy your ticket from an automatic machine at the station. This also applies to trams in the larger cities where there is a ticket machine at each tram stop.

In most German cities you can purchase a ticket which allows you to interchange between trams, underground and buses, in the one direction. (These can often be bought at tobacconists.) You an also buy a 'Rover'-ticket for a specified number of days; ask for a **TOURISTEN-FAHRKARTE** (tooristen-far-karteh) at a main statin ticket office.

WHAT TO SAY

Where does the train for (Bonn) leave from?	**Auf welchem Gleis fährt der Zug nach (Bonn) ab?**
	owf velshem glyss fairt der tsook nahk (bonn) up
At what time does the train leave for (Bonn)?	**Wann fährt der Zug nach (Bonn) ab?**
	vann fairt der tsook nahk (bonn) up
At what time does the train arrive in (Bonn)?	**Wann kommt der Zug in (Bonn) an?**
	vann kommt der tsook in (bonn) un
Is this the train for (Bonn)?	**Ist dies der Zug nach (Bonn)?**
	ist dees der tsook nahk (bonn)
Where does the bus for (Köln) leave from?	**Wo fährt der Bus nach (Köln) ab?**
	vo fairt der boos nahk (kerln) up
At what time does the bus leave for (Köln)?	**Wann fährt der Bus nach (Köln) ab?**
	vann fairt der boos nahk (kerln) up
At what time does the bus arrive at (Köln)?	**Wann kommt der Bus in (Köln) an?**
	vann kommt der boos in (kerln) un
Is this the bus for (Köln)?	**Ist dies der Bus nach (Köln)?**
	ist dees der boos nahk (kerln)
Do I have to change?	**Muss ich umsteigen?**
	moos ish oom-shtyg-en

Where does . . . leave from?	**Wo fährt . . . ab?**
	v*o* fairt . . . up
the bus	**der Bus**
	der boos
the train	**der Zug**
	der tsook
the underground	**die U–Bahn**
	dee *oo*-bahn
for the airport	**zum Flughafen**
	tsoom fl*oo*k-hahfen
for the cathedral	**zur Kathedrale/zum Dom**
	tsoor ka-teh-dr*a*hleh/tsoom d*o*me
for the beach	**zum Strand**
	tsoom shtrant
for the market place	**zum Marktplatz**
	tsoom m*a*rkt-plats
for the railway station	**zum Bahnhof**
	tsoom b*a*hn-hof
for the town centre	**zur Stadtmitte**
	tsoor sht*a*tt-mitteh
for the town hall	**zum Rathaus**
	tsoom r*a*ht-house
for St John's church	**zur Johanneskirche**
	tsoor yo-h*a*nnes-keersheh
for the swimming pool	**zum Schwimmbad**
	tsoom shv*i*mm-baht
Is this . . .	**Ist dies . . .**
	ist d*ee*s . . .
the bus for the market place?	**der Bus zum Marktplatz?**
	der b*oo*s tsoom m*a*rkt-plats
the tram for the railway station?	**die Strassenbahn zum Bahnhof?**
	dee shtr*a*hssen-bahn tsoom b*a*hn-hof
Where can I get a taxi?	**Wo kann ich ein Taxi bekommen?**
	v*o* kan ish ine t*a*xi bek*o*mmen
Can you put me off at the right stop, please?	**Können Sie mir bitte sagen, wann ich aussteigen muss?**
	k*e*rnnen zee meer b*i*tteh z*a*hg-en vann ish *o*ws-shtyg-en m*o*os
Can I book a seat?	**Kann ich einen Sitzplatz reservieren?**
	kann ish *i*nen z*i*ts-plats reserv*ee*ren

A single	**Eine einfache Fahrt**
	ineh _ine_-fak-eh _fart_
A return	**Eine Rückfahrkarte**
	ineh r_oo_k-far-karteh
First class	**Erster Klasse**
	_ai_rster kl_a_sseh
Second class	**Zweiter Klasse**
	tsv_y_-ter kl_a_sseh
One adult	**Ein Erwachsener**
	ine er-v_a_ksen-er
Two adults	**Zwei Erwachsene**
	tsv_y_ er-v_a_ksen-eh
and one child	**und ein Kind**
	oont ine k_i_nt
and two children	**und zwei Kinder**
	oont tsv_y_ k_i_n-der
How much is it?	**Wieviel kostet das?**
	v_ee_-feel k_o_stet das

LIKELY REACTIONS

Over there	**Dort drüben**
	dort dr_oo_ben
Here	**Hier**
	here
Platform (1)	**Gleis/Bahnsteig (Eins)**
	glyss/b_a_hn-shtyk (_i_nes)
At (four) o'clock	**Um (vier) Uhr**
	omm (f_ee_r) _oo_r
[_For times, see p. 131_]	
Change at (Hanover)	**Steigen Sie in (Hannover) um**
	sht_y_g-en zee in (hann-_o_fer) oom
Change at (the town hall)	**Steigen Sie am (Rathaus) um**
	sht_y_g-en zee um (r_a_ht-house) oom
This is your stop	**Hier müssen Sie aussteigen**
	here m_oo_ssen zee _o_ws-shtyg-en
There's only first class	**Es gibt nur erste Klasse**
	es geept noor _ai_rsteh kl_a_sseh
There's a supplement	**Sie müssen Zuschlag zahlen**
	zee m_oo_sen ts_oo_-shlahk ts_a_hlen

Leisure

ESSENTIAL INFORMATION

- Finding the way to a place of entertainment, see p. 19.
- For times of day, see p. 131.
- Important signs, see p. 123.
- In the more popular seaside resorts, you pay to go on the beach (**Kurtaxe**) and to hire a **Strandkorb** (shown in picture)
- Smoking is generally forbidden in theatres and cinemas. In some large cities, however, there are special cinemas for smokers (often called **SMOKY**) where you will normally have to pay more for the privilege of being free to smoke.
- It is customary to leave one's coat at the cloakroom in theatres.

WHAT TO SAY

At what time does . . . open?	**Um wieviel Uhr wird . . . geöffnet?**
	oom v*ee*feel oor veert . . . ga-*e*rffnet
the art gallery	**die Kunstgalerie**
	dee k*oo*nst-galer*ee*
the botanical garden	**der botanische Garten**
	der bot*ah*-nisheh g*a*rten
the cinema	**das Kino**
	das k*ee*-no
the concert hall	**der Konzertsaal**
	der kon-ts*ai*rt-zahl
the disco	**die Diskothek**
	dee disco-t*a*ke
the museum	**das Museum**
	das moo-z*ay*-oom
the night club	**der Nachtklub**
	der n*a*kt-kloop

the sports stadium	**das Stadion**
	das sht*a*h-dee-on
the swimming pool	**das Schwimmbad**
	das shv*i*mm-baht
the theatre	**das Theater**
	das tay-*a*hter
the zoo	**der Zoo**
	der tso
At what time does ... close?	**Um wieviel Uhr schliesst ...**
	oom v*ee*feel oor shl*ee*st ...
the art gallery	**die Kunstgalerie**
	dee k*oo*nst-galer*ee*

[See above list]

At what time does ... start?	**Um wieviel Uhr beginnt ...**
	oom v*ee*feel oor begh*i*nnt ...
the cabaret	**das Kabarett?**
	das kabar*e*tt
the concert	**das Konzert?**
	das kon-ts*ai*rt
the film	**der Film?**
	der f*i*lm
the match	**das Spiel?**
	das shp*ee*l
the play	**das Stück?**
	das sht*oo*k
the race	**das Rennen?**
	das *r*ennen
How much is it ...	**Wieviel kostet es ...**
	v*ee*feel k*o*stet es ...
for an adult?	**für einen Erwachsenen?**
	foor *i*nen er-v*a*ksen-en
for a child?	**für ein Kind?**
	for ine k*i*nt
Two adults, please	**Zwei Erwachsene, bitte**
	tsv*y* er-v*a*ksen-eh b*i*tteh
Three children, please	**Drei Kinder, bitte**
	dry k*i*n-der b*i*tteh

[State price, if there's a choice]

Stalls/circle	**Parkett/erster Rang**
	park*e*tt/*ai*rster r*u*ng

Do you have . . .	**Haben Sie . . .** h*a*hben zee . . .
a programme?	**ein Programm?** ine pro-gr*a*mm
a guide book?	**einen Führer?** inen f*oo*rer
Where's the toilet, please?	**Wo sind die Toiletten?** vo zint dee twa-l*e*tten
Where's the cloakroom?	**Wo ist die Garderobe?** vo ist dee gardeh-robeh
I would like lessons in . . .	**Ich möchte Unterricht nehmen im . . .** ish m*e*rshteh *oo*nter-risht n*a*ymen im . . .
skiing	**Skifahren** sh*ee*-fahren
sailing	**Segeln** z*a*ygeln
water skiing	**Wasserskifahren** v*a*sser-sh*ee*-fahren
wind-surfing	**Windsurfen** v*i*nd-surfen
Can I hire . . .	**Kann ich . . . leihen** kan ish . . . l*y*-en
some skis?	**Skier** sh*ee*-er
some skiboots?	**Skistiefel** sh*ee*-shteefel
a boat?	**ein Boot** ine b*o*te
a fishing rod?	**eine Angel** *i*neh *u*ng-el
a beach-chair?	**einen Strandkorb** *i*nen shtr*a*nt-korb
the necessary equipment?	**die nötige Ausrüstung** dee n*e*rtig-eh *o*ws-roostoong
How much is it . . .	**Wieviel kostet es . . .** v*ee*feel k*o*stet es . . .
per day/per hour?	**pro Tag/pro Stunde?** pro t*a*hk/pro sht*oo*ndeh
Do I need a licence?	**Brauche ich einen Erlaubnisschein?** br*o*wkeh ish *i*nen erl*o*wp-nis-shine

Asking if things are allowed

ESSENTIAL INFORMATION

- May one smoke here?
  May we smoke here?
  May I smoke here?
  Can one smoke here?
  Can I smoke here?
  Is it possible to smoke here? } **Kann man hier rauchen?**

- All these English variations can be expressed in one way in German. To save space, only the first English version: May one . . . ? is shown below.

WHAT TO SAY

Excuse me, please	**Entschuldigen Sie, bitte** ent-sh*oo*l-dig-en zee b*i*tteh
May one . . .	**Kann man . . .** k*a*nn man . . .
camp here?	**hier zelten?** here ts*e*lt-en
come in?	**hereinkommen?** hair-*i*ne-kommen
dance here?	**hier tanzen?** here t*a*ntsen
fish here?	**hier angeln?** here *u*ng-eln
get a drink here?	**hier etwas zu trinken bekommen?** here *e*tvas tsoo tr*i*nken bek*o*mmen
get out this way?	**hier hinausgehen?** here hin*o*ws-gay-en
get something to eat here?	**hier etwas zu essen bekommen?** here *e*tvas tsoo *e*ssen bek*o*mmen
leave one's things here?	**seine Sachen hier lassen?** z*i*neh z*a*k-en here lassen
look around?	**sich umsehen?** zish *oo*m-zay-en

May one ...	Kann man ...
	kann man ...
park here?	hier parken?
	here parken
picnic here?	hier picknicken?
	here pick-nicken
sit here?	sich hier hinsetzen?
	zish here hin-zetsen
smoke here?	hier rauchen?
	here rowken
swim here?	hier baden?
	here bahden
take photos here?	hier photographieren?
	here photograph-eeren
telephone here?	hier telefonieren?
	here telefon-eeren
wait here?	hier warten?
	here varten

LIKELY REACTIONS

Yes, certainly	Ja, gern(e)
	yah gairn(eh)
Help yourself	Ja, bitte
	yah bitteh
I think so	Ich glaube ja
	ish gla-oobeh yah
Of course	Natürlich
	nah-toor-lish
Yes, but be careful	Ja, aber seien Sie vorsichtig
	yah ahber zy-en zee for-zishtik
No, certainly not	Nein, auf keinen Fall
	nine owf kinen fahll
I don't think so	Ich glaube nicht
	ish gla-oobeh nisht
Not normally	Normalerweise nicht
	nor-mahler-vyzeh nisht
Sorry	Nein, tut mir leid
	nine toot meer lite

Reference

PUBLIC NOTICES

Key words on signs for drivers, pedestrians, travellers, shoppers and overnight guests.

ABFAHRT	Departures
ACHTUNG	Caution
ANKUNFT	Arrivals
ANLIEGER FREI	Access to residents only
ANMELDEFREIE WAREN	Nothing to declare
ANMELDEPFLICHTIGE WAREN	Goods to declare
ANMELDUNG	Reception
... AUF EIGENE GEFAHR	... at one's own risk
AUFZUG	Lift
AUSFAHRT	Exit (from motorway)
AUSGANG	Exit
AUSKUNFT	Information office
AUSVERKAUF	Sale, clearance sale
AUSVERKAUFT	Sold out, full house
AUTOBAHN	Motorway
BAD	Bathroom
BADEN VERBOTEN	No bathing
BAHNSTEIG	Platform
BAHNÜBERGANG	Level crossing
BAUSTELLE	Building site
BEDARFSHALTESTELLE	Bus-stop on request
BESETZT	Engaged (toilet); full (bus)
BETRETEN VERBOTEN	No trespassing
BETRIEBSFERIEN	Closed for holidays
BEWACHTER PARKPLATZ	Supervised car park
BITTE KLINGELN	Ring (bell)
BITTE KLOPFEN	Knock (door)
BITTE NICHT STÖREN	Do not disturb
BLAUE ZONE	Restricted parking zone
DAMEN	Ladies
DRÜCKEN	Push
DURCHFAHRT VERBOTEN	No through traffic
DURCHGANGSVERKEHR	Through traffic

DUSCHEN	Showers
EINBAHNSTRASSE	One-way street
EINFAHRT	Entrance, start of motorway
EINGANG	Entrance
EINORDNEN	Get in lane
EINSTIEG VORN/ HINTEN	Enter at the front/ at the rear
EINTRITT FREI	Admission free
EINWURF	Slot, put in . . .
ENDE (DER AUTOBAHN)	Motorway ends
ENGSTELLE	Road narrows
ENTWERTER	Ticket-stamping machine
ERDGESCHOSS	Ground floor
ERFRISCHUNGEN	Refreshments
ERSTE HILFE	First aid
ETAGE (ERSTE, ZWEITE, DRITTE)	Floor (first, second, third)
FAHRKARTENSCHALTER	Ticket office
FEIERTAGS GESCHLOSSEN	Closed on holidays
FERNSPRECHER	Public telephone
FEUERMELDER	Fire alarm
FREI	Vacant (toilet)
FREIBAD	Open air pool
FREMDENFÜHRER	Guide
FROSTSCHÄDEN	Road damaged by frost
FUNDBÜRO	Lost property
FUSSGÄNGERZONE	Pedestrian precinct
GEBÜHREN	Fees, charges
GEFAHR	Danger
GEFÄHRLICHE KURVE	Dangerous bend
GEFÄHRLICHE STRÖMUNGEN	Dangerous currents
GEGENVERKEHR	Two-way traffic
GEÖFFNET	Open
GEPÄCKAUF- BEWAHRUNG	Left luggage
GEPÄCKTRÄGER	Porter
GESCHLOSSEN	Closed
GESCHWINDIG- KEITSGRENZE	Speed limit
GLEIS	Platform

HALT	Halt, stop
HEISS	Hot (tap)
HERREN	Gentlemen
HÖCHSTGE-SCHWINDIGKEIT	Maximum speed
HOCHGARAGE	Multi-storey car park
HUPEN VERBOTEN	No sounding of horns
KALT	Cold (tap)
KASSE	Cash desk
KEIN DURCHGANG FÜR FUSSGÄNGER	No pedestrians
KEIN TRINKWASSER	Not for drinking
KEIN ZUTRITT	No entry
KRANKENHAUS	Hospital
KREUZUNG	Crossroads
KUNDENDIENST	Customer service
KURVENREICHE STRECKE	Winding road
LANGSAM FAHREN	Drive slowly, slow down
LAWINENGEFAHR	Avalanche area
LEBENSGEFAHR	Danger of death
LEERUNG	Collection (mail)
LICHT EINSCHALTEN	Lights on
LIEGEWAGEN	Couchette
MÜNZEINWURF	Coin to put in
MÜNZRÜCKGABE	Returned coins
NICHT BERÜHREN	Do not touch
NICHTRAUCHER	Non-smoker (compartment)
NOTAUSGANG	Emergency exit
NOTBREMSE	Emergency brake
ÖFFENTLICHE TOILETTEN	Public conveniences
ÖFFNUNGSZEITEN	Opening hours
PARKEN NUR MIT PARKSCHEIBEN	Parking discs required
PARKEN VERBOTEN	No parking
PARKPLATZ	Car park
PARTERRE	Ground floor
POLIZEI	Police
PRIVATGRUNDSTÜCK	Private grounds
RADWEG	Cycle path
RADWEG KREUZT	Cycle crossing

RAUCHEN VERBOTEN	No smoking
RAUCHER	Smoking allowed
RECHTS FAHREN	Keep right
RESERVIERT	Reserved
ROLLTREPPE	Escalator
RUHETAG	Closed all day
RUTSCHGEFAHR BEI NÄSSE	Slippery surface in damp weather
SACKGASSE	Cul-de-sac
SCHLAFWAGEN	Sleeping car, sleeper
SCHLECHTE FAHRBAHN	Bad surface (road)
SCHLIESSFÄCHER	Luggage lockers
SCHLUSSVERKAUF	(Seasonal) sale
SCHNELLDIENST	Fast service
SCHULE	School
SEITENSTREIFEN NICHT BEFAHRBAR	Soft verges
SELBSTBEDIENUNG	Self-service
SONDERANGEBOT	Special offer
SPÄTVORSTELLUNG	Late showing
SPEISEWAGEN	Dining car
SPRECHSTUNDEN	Surgery hours
STEHPLÄTZE	Standing room
STEINSCHLAG	Falling stones
STRASSENARBEITEN	Road works
STRASSENGLÄTTE	Slippery surface (road)
TIEFGARAGE	Underground car park
TIEFPARTERRE	Basement, lower ground floor
TOILETTEN	Toilet
TRINKWASSER	Drinking water
U–BAHN	Underground (train)
ÜBERHOLEN VERBOTEN	Overtaking forbidden
UMLEITUNG	Diversion
UNBEFUGTEN IST DAS BETRETEN VERBOTEN	Trespassers will be prosecuted
UNBESCHRANKTER BAHNÜBERGANG	Unguarded level crossing
VERBOTEN	Forbidden
VERKEHRSAMPELN	Traffic lights
VORFAHRT BEACHTEN	Give way
VORSICHT, BISSIGER HUND	Beware of the dog

VORSICHT VOR DEN ZÜGEN	Beware of the trains
WARTESAAL	Waiting room
WERKTAGS GEÖFFNET	Open on working days
ZIEHEN	Pull
ZIMMER FREI	Vacancies
ZIMMER ZU VERMIETEN	Room to let
ZOLL	Customs
ZUTRITT VERBOTEN	No admission
ZU VERKAUFEN	For sale
ZU VERMIETEN	For hire, to let

ABBREVIATIONS

ACS	**Automobil-Club der Schweiz**	Automobile Association of Switzerland
ADAC	**Allgemeiner Deutscher Automobil-Club**	General Automobile Association of Germany
Adr	**Adresse**	address
AG	**Aktiengesellschaft**	joint-stock company; corporation
AOK	**Allgemeine Ortskrankenkasse**	local health insurance office
AvD	**Automobil-Club von Deutschland**	Automobile Club of Germany
B	**Bundesstrasse**	A-road
Bayr	**Bayrisch**	Bavarian
Bhf	**Bahnhof**	railway station
BP	**Bundespost**	(Federal) Post Office
BRD	**Bundesrepublik Deutschland**	Federal Republic of Germany
C	**Celsius**	centigrade
DB	**Deutsche Bundesbahn**	German (Federal) Rail
DCC	**Deutscher Camping-Club**	German Camping Club
DDR	**Deutsche Demokratische Republik**	German Democratic Republic

DM	**Deutsche Mark**	German mark
DRK	**Deutsches Rotes Kreuz**	German Red Cross
DSG	**Deutsche Schlafwagen Gesellschaft**	German Sleeping Car Company
Frl	**Fräulein**	Miss
GmbH	**Gesellschaft mit beschränkter Haftpflicht**	limited company
Hbf	**Hauptbahnhof**	main railway station
JH	**Jugendherberge**	youth hostel
km	**Kilometer**	kilometre
LKW	**Lastkraftwagen**	lorry/truck
m	**Meter**	metre
Min	**Minute**	minute
MWSt	**Mehrwertsteuer**	value added tax
nachm	**nachmittags**	in the afternoon
ÖAMTC	**Österreichischer Automobil-Motorrad- und Touring-Club**	Austrian Automobile, Motorcycle and Touring Club
ÖBB	**Österreichische Bundesbahn**	Austrian (Federal) Rail
Pf(g)	**Pfennig**	pfennig
PKW	**Personenkraftwagen**	private motor car
Pl	**Platz**	(town) square
Rp	**Rappen**	Swiss centime
SB	**Selbstbedienung**	self-service
SBB	**Schweizerische Bundesbahn**	Swiss (Federal) Rail
St	**Stock**	floor, storey
Stck	**Stück**	piece, item
Std	**Stunde**	hour
Str	**Strasse**	street
tägl	**täglich**	daily
TCS	**Touring-Club der Schweiz**	Swiss Touring Club
U–Bahn	**Untergrundbahn**	underground railway
vorm	**vormittags**	in the morning
WC	**Wasser-Klosett**	toilet, lavatory

NUMBERS

Cardinal numbers

0	null	nool
1	eins	ines
2	zwei	tsvy
3	drei	dry
4	vier	feer
5	fünf	foonf
6	sechs	zex
7	sieben	zeeben
8	acht	ahkt
9	neun	noyn
10	zehn	tsain
11	elf	elf
12	zwölf	tsverlf
13	dreizehn	dry-tsain
14	vierzehn	feer-tsain
15	fünfzehn	foonf-tsain
16	sechzehn	zek-tsain
17	siebzehn	zeep-tsain
18	achtzehn	ahk-tsain
19	neunzehn	noyn-tsain
20	zwanzig	tsvan-tsik
21	einundzwanzig	ine-oont-tsvan-tsik
22	zweiundzwanzig	tsvy-oont-tsvan-tsik
23	dreiundzwanzig	dry-oont-tsvantsik
24	vierundzwanzig	feer-oont-tsvan-tsik
25	fünfundzwanzig	foonf-oont-tsvan-tsik
30	dreissig	dry-sik
35	fünfunddreissig	foonf-oont-dry-sik
36	sechsunddreissig	zex-oont-dry-sik
37	siebenunddreissig	zeeben-oont-dry-sik
38	achtunddreissig	akt-oont-dry-sik
39	neununddreissig	noyn-oont-dry-sik
40	vierzig	feer-tsik
41	einundvierzig	ine-oont-feer-tsik
50	fünfzig	foonf-tsik
51	einundfünfzig	ine-oont-foonf-tsik
60	sechzig	zek-tsik
61	einundsechzig	ine-oont-zek-tsik

70	siebzig	zeep-tsik
71	einundsiebzig	ine-oont-zeep-tsik
80	achtzig	ahk-tsik
81	einundachtzig	ine-oont-ahk-tsik
90	neunzig	noyn-tsik
91	einundneunzig	ine-oont-noyn-tsik
100	hundert	hoondert
101	hunderteins	hoondert-ines
102	hundertzwei	hoondert-tsvy
125	hundertfünfundzwanzig	hoondert-foonf-oont-tsvan-tsik
150	hundertfünfzig	hoondert-foonf-tsik
175	hundertfünfundsiebzig	hoondert-foonf-oont-zeep-tsik
200	zweihundert	tsvy-hoondert
250	zweihundertfünfzig	tsvy-hoondert-foonf-tsik
300	dreihundert	dry-hoondert
400	vierhundert	feer-hoondert
500	fünfhundert	foonf-hoondert
700	siebenhundert	zeeben-hoondert
1,000	tausend	towzent
1,100	tausendeinhundert	towzent-ine-hoondert
2,000	zweitausend	tsvy-towzent
5,000	fünftausend	foonf-towzent
10,000	zehntausend	tsain-towzent
100,000	hunderttausend	hoondert-towzent
1,000,000	eine Million	ineh mill-yon

Ordinal numbers

1st	erste	airsteh
2nd	zweite	tsvy-teh
3rd	dritte	dritteh
4th	vierte	feerteh
5th	fünfte	foonfteh
6th	sechste	zexteh
7th	siebte	zeepteh
8th	achte	ahk-teh
9th	neunte	noynteh
10th	zehnte	tsainteh
11th	elfte	elfteh
12th	zwölfte	tsverlf-teh

TIME

What time is it?	**Wie spät ist es?**
	vee shp*ai*t ist es
It's ...	**Es ist ...**
	es ist ...
one o'clock	**ein Uhr**
	*i*ne oor
two o'clock	**zwei Uhr**
	tsv*y* oor
three o'clock	**drei Uhr**
	dry oor
four o'clock	**vier Uhr**
	f*ee*r oor
in the morning	**morgens**
	m*o*rgens
in the afternoon	**nachmittags**
	n*a*hk-mittahks
in the evening	**abends**
	*a*h-bents
at night	**nachts**
	nakts
It's ...	**Es ist ...**
	es ist ...
noon	**zwölf Uhr mittags**
	tsverlf oor m*i*ttahks
midnight	**Mitternacht**
	mitter-nakt
It's ...	**Es ist ...**
	es ist ...
five past five	**fünf nach fünf**
	f*oo*nf nahk f*oo*nf
ten past five	**zehn nach fünf**
	ts*ai*n nahk f*oo*nf
a quarter past five	**viertel nach fünf**
	f*ee*rtel nahk f*oo*nf
twenty past five	**zwanzig nach fünf**
	tsv*a*n-tsik nahk f*oo*nf
twenty-five past five	**fünf vor halb sechs**
	f*oo*nf for halp zex
half past five	**halb sechs**
	halp z*e*x

It's . . .	Es ist
	es ist . . .
twenty-five to six	fünf nach halb sechs
	foonf nahk halp zex
twenty to six	zwanzig vor sechs
	tsvan-tsik for zex
a quarter to six	viertel vor sechs
	feertel for zex
ten to six	zehn vor sechs
	tsain for zex
five to six	fünf vor sechs
	foonf for zex
At what time . . . (does the train leave)?	Um wieviel Uhr . . . (fährt der Zug ab)?
	oom veefeel oor (fairt der tsook up)
At . . .	Um . . .
	oom . . .
13.00	dreizehn Uhr
	dry-tsain oor
14.05	vierzehn Uhr fünf
	feer-tsain oor foonf
15.10	fünfzehn Uhr zehn
	foonf-tsain oor tsain
16.15	sechzehn Uhr fünfzehn
	zek-tsain oor foonf-tsain
17.20	siebzehn Uhr zwanzig
	zeep-tsain oor tsvan-tsik
18.25	achtzehn Uhr fünfundzwanzig
	ak-tsain oor foonf-oon-tsvan-tsik
19.30	neunzehn Uhr dreissig
	noyn-tsain oor dry-sik
20.35	zwanzig Uhr fünfunddreissig
	tsvan-tsik oor foonf-oon-dry-sik
21.40	einundzwanzig Uhr vierzig
	ine-oon-tsvan-tsik oor feer-tsik
22.45	zweiundzwanzig Uhr fünfundvierzig
	tsvy-oon-tsvan-tsik oor foonf-oon-feer-tsik
23.50	dreiundzwanzig Uhr fünfzig
	dry-oon-tsvan-tsik oor foonf-tsik
0.55	null Uhr fünfundfünfzig
	nool oor foonf-oon-foonf-tsik

in ten minutes	**in zehn Minuten**
	in tsain minooten
in a quarter of an hour	**in einer Viertelstunde**
	in iner feertel-shtoondeh
in half an hour	**in einer halben Stunde**
	in iner halben shtoondeh
in three quarters of an hour	**in einer Dreiviertelstunde**
	in iner dry-feertel-shtoondeh

DAYS

Monday	**Montag**
	mone-tahk
Tuesday	**Dienstag**
	deens-tahk
Wednesday	**Mittwoch**
	mitt-vok
Thursday	**Donnerstag**
	donners-tahk
Friday	**Freitag**
	fry-tahk
Saturday	**Samstag/Sonnabend**
	zams-tahk/zonn-ahbent
Sunday	**Sonntag**
	zonn-tahk
last Monday	**letzten Montag**
	lets-ten mone-tahk
next Tuesday	**nächsten Dienstag**
	nexten deens-tahk
on Wednesday	**(am) Mittwoch**
	(um) mit-vok
on Thursdays	**donnerstags**
	donners-tahks
until Friday	**bis Freitag**
	bis fry-tahk
before Saturday	**vor Samstag/Sonnabend**
	for zams-tahk/zonn-ahbent
after Sunday	**nach Sonntag**
	nahk zonn-tahk
the day before yesterday	**vorgestern**
	for-ghestern

two days ago	**vor zwei Tagen**
	for tsv*y* t*a*hg-en
yesterday	**gestern**
	gh*e*stern
yesterday morning	**gestern morgen**
	gh*e*stern m*o*rgen
yesterday afternoon	**gestern nachmittag**
	gh*e*stern n*a*hk-mittahk
last night	**gestern abend**
	gh*e*stern *a*hbent
today	**heute**
	h*oy*-teh
this morning	**heute morgen**
	hoy-teh m*o*rgen
this afternoon	**heute nachmittag**
	hoy-teh n*a*hk-mittahk
tonight	**heute abend**
	hoy-teh *a*hbent
tomorrow	**morgen**
	m*o*rgen
tomorrow morning	**morgen früh**
	morgen fr*oo*
tomorrow afternoon	**morgen nachmittag**
	morgen n*a*hk-mittahk
tomorrow evening	**morgen abend**
	morgen *a*hbent
tomorrow night	**morgen abend**
	morgen *a*hbent
the day after tomorrow	**übermorgen**
	*oo*ber-morgen

MONTHS AND DATES

January	**Januar**
	y*a*h-noo-ahr
February	**Februar**
	f*ay*-broo-ahr
March	**März**
	mairts
April	**April**
	ah-pr*i*l

May	**Mai**
	my
June	**Juni**
	yoo-nee
July	**Juli**
	yoo-lee
August	**August**
	ow-goost
September	**September**
	zeptember
October	**Oktober**
	oktober
November	**November**
	november
December	**Dezember**
	detsember
in January	**im Januar**
	im yah-noo-ahr
until February	**bis Februar**
	bis fay-broo-ahr
before March	**vor März**
	for mairts
after April	**nach April**
	nahk ah-pril
during May	**im Mai**
	im my
not until June	**nicht vor Juni**
	nisht for yoo-nee
the beginning of July	**Anfang Juli**
	anfang yoo-lee
the middle of August	**Mitte August**
	mitteh ow-goost
the end of September	**Ende September**
	endeh zeptember
last month	**(im) letzten Monat**
	(im) letsten monaht
this month	**diesen Monat**
	deezen monaht
next month	**nächsten Monat**
	nexten monaht
in spring	**im Frühling/ Frühjahr**
	im frooling/froo-yar

in summer	**im Sommer** im *zommer*
in autumn	**im Herbst** im h*ai*rpst
in winter	**im Winter** im *vi*nter
this year	**dieses Jahr** d*ee*zes yar
last year	**letztes Jahr** *le*tstes yar
next year	**nächstes Jahr** n*e*xtes yar
in 1982	**neunzehnhundertzweiundachtzig** n*oy*n-tsain-hoondert tsv*y*-oont-ahk-tsik
in 1985	**neunzehnhundertfünfundachtzig** n*oy*n-tsain-hoondert f*oo*nf-oont-ahk-tsik
in 1990	**neunzehnhundertneunzig** n*oy*n-tsain-hoondert n*oy*n-tsik
What's the date today?	**Welches Datum haben wir heute?** velshes d*ah*-toom h*ah*ben veer h*oy*-teh
It's the 6th of March	**Heute ist der sechste März** h*oy*-teh ist der *ze*xteh m*ai*rts
It's the 12th of April	**Heute ist der zwölfte April** h*oy*-teh ist der tsverlf-teh ah-pr*i*l
It's the 21st of August	**Heute ist der einundzwanzigste August** h*oy*-teh ist der *i*ne-oont-tsvansix-teh ow-g*oo*st

Public holidays

Unless otherwise specified, offices, shops and schools are closed on these days in Austria, Germany and Switzerland.

1 January	**Neujahrstag**	New Year's Day
6 January	**Dreikönigsfest**	Epiphany (Austria only)
...	**Karfreitag**	Good Friday (Germany and Switzerland)
...	**Ostermontag**	Easter Monday
1 May	**Tag der Arbeit**	Labour Day (Austria and Germany)
...	**Himmelfahrt**	Ascension

...	**Pfingstmontag**	Whit Monday
...	**Fronleichnam**	Corpus Christi (Austria and some regions of Germany)
17 June	**Siebzehnter Juni**	Day of Unity (Germany)
15 August	**Mariä Himmelfahrt**	Assumption Day (Austria)
26 October	**Nationalfeiertag**	National Day (Austria)
1 November	**Allerheiligen**	All Saints Day (Austria)
...	**Buss-und Bettag**	Day of Prayer and Repentance (Germany)
8 December	**die unbefleckte Empfängnis**	Immaculate Conception (Austria)
24 December	**Heiligabend**	Christmas Eve (half day)
25 December	**erster Weihnachtstag**	Christmas Day
26 December	**zweiter Weihnachtstag**	Boxing Day
26 December	**Stephanstag**	St Stephen's Day (Austria and Switzerland)

COUNTRIES AND NATIONALITIES

Countries

Australia	**Australien** owstr*a*h-lee-en
Austria	**Österreich** *er*ster-rike
Belgium	**Belgien** b*e*lg-ee-en
Britain	**Grossbritannien** gross-brit*a*hn-ee-en
Canada	**Kanada** k*a*nadah
Czechoslovakia	**die Tschechoslowakei** dee czechoslovak-*y*
East Africa	**Ostafrika** ost-*a*frikah
East Germany	**die DDR** dee d*e*h-deh-*ai*r
Eire	**Irland** *ee*r-lant

England	**England** *eng*-lant
France	**Frankreich** *frank*-rysh
Greece	**Griechenland** *gree*shen-lant
India	**Indien** *ind*-ee-en
Italy	**Italien** it*ahl*-ee-en
Luxembourg	**Luxemburg** *loo*xem-boork
Netherlands	**Holland** *hollant
New Zealand	**Neuseeland** noy-*zay*-lant
Northern Ireland	**Nordirland** nort-*eer*-lant
Pakistan	**Pakistan** p*ah*-kistahn
Poland	**Polen** *pohl*-en
Portugal	**Portugal** port-oo-*gahl*
Scotland	**Schottland** sh*ot*-lant
South Africa	**Südafrika** zood-*afrikah
Spain	**Spanien** shp*ah*-nee-en
Switzerland	**die Schweiz** dee shvyts
to/for Switzerland	**in die Schweiz** in dee shvyts
in Switzerland	**in der Schweiz** in der shvyts
United States	**die Vereinigten Staaten** dee fer-*ine*-nikten sht*ah*ten
to/for the United States	**in die Vereinigten Staaten** in dee fer-*ine*-nikten sht*ah*ten
in the United States	**in den Vereinigten Staaten** in den fer-*ine*-nikten sht*ah*ten
USSR	**die UdSSR** dee oo-deh-es-es-*air*

in/to/for the USSR	[*as Switzerland*]
Wales	**Wales**
	wales
West Germany	**Westdeutschland**
	vest-doytsh-lant
West Indies	**Westindien**
	vest-*i*nd-ee-en
Yugoslavia	**Jugoslawien**
	yoogo-sl*a*hv-ee-en

Nationalities

[*Use the first alternative for men, the second for women*]

American	**Amerikaner/Amerikanerin**
	ameri-k*a*h-ner/ameri-k*a*h-ner-in
Australian	**Australier/Australierin**
	owstr*a*h-lee-er/owstr*a*h-lee-er-in
British	**Brite/Britin**
	breeteh/breetin
Canadian	**Kanadier/Kanadierin**
	kan*a*h-dee-er/kan*a*h-dee-er-in
East African	**Ostafrikaner/Ostafrikanerin**
	ost-afrik*a*h-ner/
	ost-afrik*a*h-ner-in
English	**Engländer/Engländerin**
	eng-lender/eng-lender-in
Indian	**Inder/Inderin**
	*i*nder/inder-in
Irish	**Ire/Irin**
	*ee*reh/*ee*rin
a New Zealander	**Neuseeländer/Neuseeländerin**
	noy-z*a*y-lender/noy-z*a*y-lender-in
a Pakistani	**Pakistaner/Pakistanerin**
	paki-st*a*hn-er/paki-st*a*hn-er-in
Scots	**Schotte/Schottin**
	shotteh/sh*o*ttin
South African	**Südafrikaner/Südafrikanerin**
	zood-afrik*a*h-ner/
	zood-afrik*a*h-ner-in
Welsh	**Waliser/Waliserin**
	vah-l*ee*zer/vah-l*ee*zer-in
West Indian	**Westinder/Westinderin**
	vest-*i*nder/vest-*i*nder-in

DEPARTMENT STORE GUIDE

Absatz-Bar	Heel bar
Alles für das Kind	Children's department
Auskunft	Information
Aussteuerartikel	Bridal room
Babyausstattung	Layette
Babynahrung	Baby food
Bastelabteilung	Do-it-yourself
Bettwäsche	Bedding, linen
Bilder und Rahmen	Paintings and frames
Blusen	Blouses
Brot	Bread
Bücher	Books
Büroartikee	Office supplies
Camping	Camping
Damenhüte	Millinery
Damenkonfektion/bekleidung	Ladies fashions
Damenwäsche	Lingerie
Delikatessen	Delicatessen
Dritte	Third
Elektrowaren	Electric appliances
Erdgeschoss	Ground floor
Erfrischungsraum	Refreshments
Erste	First
Etage	Floor
Fahrstühle	Lifts
Feinfrost	Frozen food
Fernsehen	Television
Frischfleisch	Fresh meat
Frisör	Hairdresser
Gardinen	Curtains
Geflügel	Poultry
Gemüse	Vegetables
Geschenkartikel	Gifts
Glas	Glassware
Haushaltswaren	Household goods
Heimwerker	DIY
Herrenartikel	Men(s)
Herrenkonfektion/bekleidung	Menswear
Kinderkonfektion/bekleidung	Children's clothes
Kosmetikartikel	Cosmetics
Kücheneinrichtung	Kitchen furniture
Kurzwaren	Haberdashery
Lampen	Lamps

Lebensmittel	Food
Lederwaren	Leather goods
Miederwaren	Girdles
Möbel	Furniture
Nähmaschinen	Sewing-machines
Oberhemden	Shirts (department)
Obst	Fresh fruit
Parfümerie	Perfumery
Pelze	Furs
Photoartikel	Photography
Porzellan	China
Putzmittel	Cleaning materials
Radio	Radio
Reisebüro	Travel agency
Rolltreppen	Escalators
Schallplatten	Records
Schmuck	Jewellery
Schnellimbiss	Snack bar
Schnittmuster	Paper patterns
Schreibwaren	Stationery
Schuhe	Shoes
Spielwaren	Toys
Spirituosen	Spirits, liquors
Sportartikel	Sports articles
Stock	Floor
Stoffe	Fabrics, drapery
Strickwaren	Knitwear
Strümpfe	Stockings
Süsswaren	Sweets
Tabakwaren	Tobacco
Teppiche	Carpets
Tiefgeschoss	Basement
Toilettenartikel	Toiletries
Trikotagen	Hosiery
Umtauschkasse	Exchange and refund
Untergeschoss	Basement
Vierte	Fourth
Weine	Wine
Werkzeuge	Tools
Wolle	Wool
Wurstwaren	Cold meats
Zeitungen	Newspapers
Zoo	Zoo
Zweite	Second

CONVERSION TABLES

Read the centre column of these tables from right to left to convert
from metric to imperial and from left to right to convert from
imperial to metric e.g. 5 litres = 8.80 pints; 5 pints = 2.84 litres.

pints		litres	gallons		litres
1.76	1	0.57	0.22	1	4.55
3.52	2	1.14	0.44	2	9.09
5.28	3	1.70	0.66	3	13.64
7.07	4	2.27	0.88	4	18.18
8.80	5	2.84	1.00	5	22.73
10.56	6	3.41	1.32	6	27.28
12.32	7	3.98	1.54	7	31.82
14.08	8	4.55	1.76	8	36.37
15.84	9	5.11	1.98	9	40.91

ounces		grams	pounds		kilos
0.04	1	28.35	2.20	1	0.45
0.07	2	56.70	4.41	2	0.91
0.11	3	85.05	6.61	3	1.36
0.14	4	113.40	8.82	4	1.81
0.18	5	141.75	11.02	5	2.27
0.21	6	170.10	13.23	6	2.72
0.25	7	198.45	15.43	7	3.18
0.28	8	226.80	17.64	8	3.63
0.32	9	255.15	19.84	9	4.08

inches		centimetres	yards		metres
0.39	1	2.54	1.09	1	0.91
0.79	2	5.08	2.19	2	1.83
1.18	3	7.62	3.28	3	2.74
1.58	4	10.16	4.37	4	3.66
1.17	5	12.70	5.47	5	4.57
2.36	6	15.24	6.56	6	5.49
2.76	7	17.78	7.66	7	6.40
3.15	8	20.32	8.65	8	7.32
3.54	9	22.86	9.84	9	8.23

miles		kilometres
0.62	1	1.61
1.24	2	3.22
1.86	3	4.83
2.49	4	6.44
3.11	5	8.05
3.73	6	9.66
4.35	7	11.27
4.97	8	12.87
5.59	9	14.48

A quick way to convert kilometres to miles: divide by 8 and multiply by 5. To convert miles to kilometres: divide by 5 and multiply by 8.

fahrenheit (°F)	centigrade (°C)		lbs/ sq in	k/ sq cm
212°	100°	boiling point	18	1.3
100°	38°		20	1.4
98.4°	36.9°	body temperature	22	1.5
86°	30°		25	1.7
77°	25°		29	2.0
68°	20°		32	2.3
59°	15°		35	2.5
50°	10°		36	2.5
41°	5°		39	2.7
32°	0°	freezing point	40	2.8
14°	−10°		43	3.0
−4°	−20°		45	3.2
			46	3.2
			50	3.5
			60	4.2

To convert °C to °F: divide by 5, multiply by 9 and add 32. To convert °F to °C: take away 32, divide by 9 and multiply by 5.

CLOTHING SIZES

Remember – always try on clothes before buying. Clothing sizes are usually unreliable.

women's dresses and suits

Europe	38	40	42	44	46	48
UK	32	34	36	38	40	42
USA	10	12	14	16	18	20

men's suits and coats

Europe	46	48	50	52	54	56
UK and USA	36	38	40	42	44	46

men's shirts

Europe	36	37	38	39	41	42	43
UK and USA	14	14½	15	15½	16	16½	17

socks

Europe	38–39	39–40	40–41	41–42	42–43
UK and USA	9½	10	10½	11	11½

shoes

Europe	34	35½	36½	38	39	41	42	43	44	45
UK	2	3	4	5	6	7	8	9	10	11
USA	3½	4½	5½	6½	7½	8½	9½	10½	11½	12½

Do it yourself

Some notes on the language

This section does not deal with 'grammar' as such. The purpose here is to explain some of the most obvious and elementary nuts and bolts of the language, based on the principal phrases included in the book. This information should enable you to produce numerous sentences of your own making. There is no pronunciation guide in most of this section partly because it would get in the way of the explanations and partly because you have to do it yourself at this stage if you are serious: work out the pronunciation from all the earlier examples in the book.

THE

All nouns in German belong to one of three genders: masculine, feminine or neuter, irrespective of whether they refer to living beings or inanimate objects.

The	masculine	feminine	neuter
the address		die Adresse	
the apple	der Apfel		
the bill		die Rechnung	
the cup of tea		die Tasse Tee	
the glass of beer			das Glas Bier
the key	der Schlüssel		
the luggage			das Gepäck
the menu		die Speisekarte	
the newspaper		die Zeitung	
the receipt		die Quittung	
the ham sandwich			das Schinkenbrot
the suitcase	der Koffer		
the telephone directory			das Telefonbuch
the timetable	der Fahrplan		

plural

die Adressen	the addresses
die Äpfel	the apples
die Rechnungen	the bills
die Tassen Tee	the cups of tea
die Gläser Bier	the glasses of beer
die Schlüssel	the keys
die Speisekarten	the menus
die Zeitungen	the newspapers
die Quittungen	the receipts
die Schinkenbrote	the ham sandwiches
die Koffer	the suitcases
die Telefonbücher	the telephone directories
die Fahrpläne	the timetables

Important things to remember

- There is no way of predicting if a noun is masculine, feminine or neuter. You just have to learn and remember its gender. Nouns ending in -ung, -keit and -heit are feminine and nouns ending in -chen or -lein are neuter, but this sort of rule is not very helpful because it accounts for relatively few words.
- In the tables, *the* is der before masculine nouns, die before feminine nouns, das before neuter nouns.
- Does it matter? Not unless you want to make a serious attempt to speak correctly and scratch beneath the surface of the language. You would be understood if you said das Speisekarte or die Fahrplan, providing your pronunciation was good.
- In the word list *the* is die before any noun in the plural (not to be confused with the feminine).
- There is no easy way of remembering how to spell German nouns in the plural. (To get into the right frame of mind, think of the plural of *ox*, *goose* and *sheep* in English.) Here are the six ways of making a noun plural:
    add -en, -n, or -nen
    change a vowel sound by putting on an umlaut ä, ö, ü
    don't add anything to the end
    add -er, usually with an umlaut on an a, o or u
    add -e, often with an umlaut on an a, o or u
    add -s to an imported foreign word like Hotel

• The methods are easy enough, but knowing which method to apply to which noun is a different matter. In this section, however, the spelling of nouns in the plural are given for you: try to learn them by heart as you meet and practise them.

Practise saying and writing these sentences in German:

Where is the key?	**Wo ist der Schlüssel?**
Where is the receipt?	**Wo ist . . . ?**
Where is the address?	
Where is the luggage?	
Where are the keys?	**Wo sind die Schlüssel?**
Where are the ham sandwiches?	**Wo sind . . . ?**
Where are the newspapers?	
Where are the apples?	

Now make up more sentences along the same lines. Try adding *please*: **bitte**, at the beginning or end.

! CAUTION
In phrases beginning
Have you got the . . . ?
I'd like the . . .
Where can I get the . . . ?
masculine singular nouns (e.g. apple, key, suitcase, timetable) pose a problem. Quite simply, the word for *the*: **der** has to change to **den**. (This is usually called the Accusative Case, but it affects only the masculine singular.) In the Accusative Case
der Apfel becomes **den Apfel**
der Schlüssel becomes **den Schlüssel**
der Koffer becomes **den Koffer**
der Fahrplan becomes **den Fahrplan**
(The plural is not affected)

Practise saying and writing these sentences in German. (Look out for the caution sign !)

! Have you got the key?	**Haben Sie den Schlüssel?**
! Have you got the suitcase?	**Haben Sie . . . ?**
Have you got the luggage?	
Have you got the telephone directory?	
Have you got the menu?	

! I'd like the key   **Ich möchte . . . Schlüssel**
! I'd like the timetable
  I'd like the bill
  I'd like the receipt
  I'd like the keys
! Where can I get the key?   **Wo kann man . . . Schlüssel**
                                  bekommen?

  Where can I get the address?
  Where can I get the timetables?

Now make up more sentences along the same lines.
Try adding *please*: **bitte**, at the beginning or end.

A/AN

A/an	masculine	feminine	neuter
an address		eine Adresse	
an apple	ein Apfel		
a bill		eine Rechnung	
a cup of tea		eine Tasse Tee	
a glass of beer			ein Glas Bier
a key	ein Schlüssel		
a menu		eine Speisekarte	
a newspaper		eine Zeitung	
a receipt		eine Quittung	
a ham sandwich			ein Schinkenbrot
a suitcase	ein Koffer		
a telephone directory			ein Telefonbuch
a timetable	ein Fahrplan		

plural	Some/any
Adressen	addresses
Äpfel	apples
Rechnungen	bills
Tassen Tee	cups of tea
Gläser Bier	glasses of beer
Schlüssel	keys
Speisekarten	menus
Zeitungen	newspapers
Quittungen	receipts
Schinkenbrote	ham sandwiches
Koffer	suitcases
Telefonbücher	telephone directories
Fahrpläne	timetables

Important things to remember

- In the tables, *a* or *an* is **ein** before a masculine noun, **eine** before a feminine noun, **ein** before a neuter noun.
- *Some* or *any* before a noun in the plural has no equivalent in German. Just leave it out.

! CAUTION

In phrases beginning
Have you got . . . ?
I'd like . . .
Where can I get . . . ?
Is there . . . ?
Are there . . . ?
I'll have . . .
I need . . .
masculine singular nouns pose a problem. The word for *a/an*: **ein** has to change to **einen**. In these examples (of the Accusative Case) only masculine singular nouns are affected
ein Apfel becomes **einen** Apfel
ein Schlüssel becomes **einen** Schlüssel
ein Koffer becomes **einen** Koffer
ein Fahrplan becomes **einen Fahrplan**
(The plural is not affected.)

Practise saying and writing these sentences in German. (Look out for the caution sign !)

Have you got a receipt?	**Haben Sie eine ... ?**
! Have you got an apple?	
I'd like a telephone directory	**Ich möchte ein ...**
! I'd like a timetable	
I'd like (some) ham sandwiches	
Where can I get a cup of tea?	**Wo kann man eine ...** **bekommen?**
! Where can I get a suitcase?	
Where can I get (some) newspapers?	
Is there a menu?	**Gibt es hier eine ... ?**
! Is there a key?	**Gibt es hier ... ?**
! Is there a timetable?	
Are there (any) keys?	**Gibt es hier ... ?**
Are there (any) newspapers?	
Are there (any) ham sandwiches?	
I'll have a glass of beer	**Ich hätte gern ein ...**
I'll have a cup of tea	**Ich hätte gern ...**
! I'll have an apple	
I'll have (some) apples	
I'll have (some) ham sandwiches	
I need a receipt	**Ich brauche eine ...**
! I need a suitcase	
I need a cup of tea	
! I need a key	
I need (some) suitcases	
I need (some) addresses	
I need (some) ham sandwiches	

Now make up more sentences along the same lines.

SOME/ANY

In cases where *some* or *any* refer to more than one thing, such as *some/any newspapers* and *some/any tomatoes*, there is no German equivalent, as explained earlier:

Zeitungen	some/any newspapers
Tomaten	some/any tomatoes

As a guide, you can usually count the number of containers or whole items.

In cases where *some* refers to part of a whole thing or an indefinite quantity, the word etwas can be used. Neither the gender of the noun nor the Accusative Case pose problems. Look at the list below and complete it:

the butter	die Butter	etwas Butter	some butter
the bread	das Brot	etwas Brot	some bread
the cheese	der Käse	etwas Käse	some cheese
the coffee	der Kaffee	etwas Kaffee	some coffee
the ice-cream	das Eis	...	some ice-cream
the lemonade	die Limonade	...	some lemonade
the pineapple	die Ananas	...	some pineapple
the sugar	der Zucker	...	some sugar
the tea	der Tee	...	some tea
the water	das Wasser	...	some water
the wine	der Wein	...	some wine

(Etwas is not essential, however, and can just be left out altogether.)

Practise saying and writing these sentences in German:

| Have you got some coffee? | Haben Sie etwas Kaffee? |
| | Haben Sie Kaffee? |

Have you got some ice-cream?
Have you got some pineapple?
I'd like some butter.
I'd like some sugar.
I'd like some bread.
Where can I get some cheese?
Where can I get some ice-cream?
Where can I get some water?
Is there any lemonade?
Is there any water?
Is there any wine?
I'll have some butter.
I'll have some tea.
I'll have some coffee.
I need some sugar.
I need some butter.
I need some coffee.

THIS AND THAT

There are two words in German
dies (this)
das (that)
If you don't know the German name for an object, just point and say:

Ich möchte das	I'd like that
Ich hätte gern dies	I'll have this
Ich brauche das	I need that

HELPING OTHERS

You can help yourself with phrases such as:

I'd like . . . a ham sandwich	**Ich möchte . . . ein Schinkenbrot**
Where can I get . . . a cup of tea?	**Wo kann man . . . eine Tasse Tee . . . bekommen?**
I'll have . . . a glass of beer	**Ich hätte gern . . . ein Glas Bier**
I need . . . a receipt	**Ich brauche . . . eine Quittung**

If you come across a compatriot having trouble making himself or herself understood, you should be able to speak to a German person on their behalf.

He'd like . . .	**Er möchte ein Schinkenbrot** er mershteh *i*ne sh*i*nken-brote
She'd like . . .	**Sie möchte ein Schinkenbrot** zee mershteh *i*ne sh*i*nken-brote

Strictly speaking, **kann man . . . ?** means *can one . . . ?* and normally serves instead of *can I. . . ?* (kann ich. . . ?), *can he. . . ?*, *can she. . . ?*, *can they. . . ?* and *can we. . . ?* However, all the above-mentioned variations in German are included in the remainder of this section because of their potential usefulness.

Where can he get . . . ?	**Wo kann er eine Tasse Tee bekommen?** vo kann er *i*neh t*a*sseh tay bek*o*mmen
Where can she get . . . ?	**Wo kann sie eine Tasse Tee bekommen?** vo kann zee *i*neh t*a*sseh tay bek*o*mmen
He'll have . . .	**Er hätte gern ein Glas Bier** er hetteh g*ai*rn *i*ne glass beer

She'll have ...	**Sie hätte gern ein Glas Bier** zee hetteh ga*i*rn *i*ne glass b*ee*r
He needs ...	**Er braucht eine Quittung** er br*a-oo*kt *i*neh kv*i*ttoong
She needs ...	**Sie braucht eine Quittung** zee br*a-oo*kt *i*neh kv*i*ttoong

You can also help a couple or a group if *they* are having difficulties. The German word for *they* is also sie, but there is a difference, which is fairly easy to detect. (Elsewhere in this book you will have noticed that Sie can also mean *you*)

They'd like ...	**Sie möchten (etwas) Käse** zee m*e*rshten (*e*tvas) k*ay*-zeh
Where can they get ... ?	**Wo können sie (etwas) Butter bekommen?** v*o* k*e*rnen zee (*e*tvas) b*oo*tter bekommen
They'll have ...	**Sie hätten gern (etwas) Wein** zee hetten ga*i*rn (*e*tvas) v*i*ne
They need ...	**Sie brauchen (etwas) Wasser** zee br*a-oo*ken (*e*tvas) v*a*sser

What about the two of you? No problem the word for *we* is **wir.**

We'd like ...	**Wir möchten (etwas)Wein** veer m*e*rshten (*e*tvas) v*i*ne
Where can we get ... ?	**Wo können wir (etwas) Wasser bekommen?** v*o* k*e*rnen veer (*e*tvas) v*a*sser bekommen
We'll have ...	**Wir hätten gern (etwas) Butter** veer hetten ga*i*rn (*e*tvas) b*oo*tter
We need ...	**Wir brauchen (etwas) Zucker** veer br*a-oo*ken (*e*tvas) ts*oo*cker

Try writing out your own checklist for these four useful phrase-starters, like this:

Ich möchte ...	Wir möchten ...
Er möchte ...	Sie möchten ...
Sie möchte ...	

Wo kann ich ... bekommen?	Wo ... wir ... ?
Wo kann er ... bekommen?	Wo ... sie ... ?
Wo ... sie ... bekommen?	

MORE PRACTICE

Here are some more German names of things. See how many
different sentences you can make up, using the various points of
information given earlier in this section.

		singular	plural
1	ashtray	Aschenbecher (m)	Aschenbecher
2	ballpen	Kugelschreiber (m)	Kugelschreiber
3	bag	Tasche (f)	Taschen
4	bottle	Flasche (f)	Flaschen
5	car	Auto (n)	Autos
6	cigarette	Zigarette (f)	Zigaretten
7	corkscrew	Korkenzieher (m)	Korkenzieher
8	egg	Ei (n)	Eier
9	house	Haus (n)	Häuser
10	knife	Messer (n)	Messer
11	mountain	Berg (m)	Berge
12	plate	Teller (m)	Teller
13	postcard	Postkarte (f)	Postkarten
14	room	Zimmer (n)	Zimmer
15	shoe	Schuh (m)	Schuhe
16	stamp	Briefmarke (f)	Briefmarken
17	street	Strasse (f)	Strassen
18	ticket	Fahrkarte (f)	Fahrkarten
19	train	Zug (m)	Züge
20	wallet	Brieftasche (f)	Brieftaschen

Index

Arthur Eperon
Traveller's France

Six major routes across France, taking in the best restaurants and hotels, visiting the most interesting out-of-the-way places. This detailed and up-to-the-minute handbook is for the traveller who wants more out of France than a mad dash down the motorway. Each of the six routes across the country is illustrated with a specially-commissioned two-colour map, and includes a host of information on where to eat and drink, where to take children, where to stay, and how to get the most out of the towns and countryside.

Travellers' Italy

A whole variety of holiday routes to guarantee that you eat, drink, explore and relax in the places the Italians themselves would choose. The best places to sample local speciality foods and wines, spectacular scenery, facts the history books won't tell you, as well as the magnificent beaches and art treasures you'd expect. Arthur Eperon is one of the best-known travel writers in Europe and has an extensive knowledge of Italy and its food and wine. With an introduction by Frank Bough.

Ken Welsh
Hitch-Hiker's Guide to Europe

The new and completely updated edition of this invaluable guide covers Europe, North Africa and the Middle East. Ken Welsh gives advice on routes to take, what to take, eating, sleeping, local transport, what to see, together with information on currency, useful phrases and working abroad.

'Hitch-hikers will adopt it as their travelling bible but it's amusing and informative for those who fancy more traditional ways'   BBC

edited by Harriet Peacock
The Alternative Holiday Catalogue

If you're looking for a holiday that you won't find in a travel agent's window . . . if there's something you've always wanted to try your hand at . . . or if you want to take your special interest on holiday with you, this A-to-Z of ideas and information is the book you need. 150 different types of special interest holiday, from backgammon and Bible-study to Zen, upholstery and giving up smoking. This book tells you where to go, what to take, what it costs, and what you'll find when you get there.

John Slater
Just Off the Motorway

The new and enlarged edition of a sensational bestseller. Introduction by Russell Harty.

Here's the new, bang-up-to-date edition of the handbook everyone needs. Detailed research, careful sampling, and more than 150 maps show where you can find any service you require – cheaper and better – by turning off at a junction and driving no more than three miles off the motorway – eating, drinking, overnight stops, breakdown services, petrol, visits.

'Worth a detour to buy it'   DAILY MAIL

Just Off for the Weekend
Slater's hotel guide

The bestselling author of *Just Off the Motorway* has selected more than a hundred places to stay, with details of what to see and walks to take, specially recommended pubs and restaurants – and all within a Friday evening's drive from one of England's big cities. With an introduction by Anna Ford.